Everything You Always Wanted To Know

ABOUT THE SYMPHONY ORCHESTRA

A Handbook For Concertgoers

by Lucas Drew and Raymond Barr

Everything You Always Wanted to Know
About The Symphony Orchestra
(second printing, revised version)

Published by Edwin F. Kalmus & Co., Inc.
Printed by The Well-Tempered Press, Inc.
a subsidiary of
Edwin F. Kalmus & Co., Inc.

First printing September, 1990
Second printing September, 1992
Catalog # A7808
ISBN 0-913402-05-2

Everything You Always Wanted To Know
ABOUT THE SYMPHONY ORCHESTRA
by Lucas Drew and Raymond Barr

Edwin F. Kalmus & Co., Inc.
6403 West Rogers Circle
Boca Raton, Florida 33487
ph. (407) 241-6340
fax 407-241-6347

Everything You Always Wanted To Know

ABOUT THE SYMPHONY ORCHESTRA

A Handbook For Concertgoers

by Lucas Drew and Raymond Barr

EDWIN F. KALMUS & CO., INC. ● BOCA RATON ● 1990

ACKNOWLEDGEMENTS

The authors gratefully acknowledge the assistance of the following colleagues in the preparation of this book:

Clark McAlister, Editor in Chief, Edwin F. Kalmus, Inc.

Jody Atwood, Editor, *The American String Teacher*

BoldType, Inc., Typography
Sandra Mesics, Book Design
Greta West, Typing

Members of the staff of The Philadelphia Orchestra
Bernard Jacobson
Jean Brubaker
Phyllis Susen
Judith Karp Kurnick

The Instrumentalist
David C. Hunt
Ron Berg

Riverrun Press, Inc.

Spectrum Music Press—"Spectrum Seals of Great Composers,"
Fred Gong, Artist

Diana Andersen , Philharmonic Orchestra of Florida
Shawn Coughlin, Illustrations
Matthew Gannon, Graphic Designs

TABLE OF CONTENTS

Preface

**1. 95 QUESTIONS YOU ALWAYS WANTED TO ASK
ABOUT THE SYMPHONY ORCHESTRA**   **1**
   ABOUT THE CONCERT AND THE ORCHESTRA   1
   THE CONDUCTOR   9
   ORCHESTRAL MUSICIANS AND THEIR INSTRUMENTS   13
   THE ORGANIZATION AND ROUTINE OF A
        SYMPHONY ORCHESTRA   18
   MISCELLANEOUS   20

2. THE DEVELOPMENT OF THE ORCHESTRA   **23**
   BAROQUE PERIOD   23
   CLASSICAL PERIOD   24
   NINETEENTH CENTURY   25
   TWENTIETH CENTURY   27
   SUMMARY—EIGHTEENTH-TWENTIETH CENTURY   28

3. THE INSTRUMENTS OF THE ORCHESTRA   **29**
   STRING INSTRUMENTS   29
     Violin   29
     Viola   31
     Violoncello (Cello)   31
     Double Bass   34
     Harp   34
     Guitar   35
   WIND INSTRUMENTS   35
     Non-reed Woodwinds   36
       Flute   36
       Piccolo   36
     Single-reed Woodwinds   36
       Clarinet   36
       Bass Clarinet   37

Saxophone	37
Double-reed Woodwinds	38
Oboe	38
English Horn	39
Bassoon	42
Contrabassoon	42
BRASS INSTRUMENTS	43
Trumpet	43
French Horn	44
Trombone	45
Tuba	45
PERCUSSION INSTRUMENTS	49
Drum-type Instruments	49
Kettledrums (Timpani)	49
Bass Drum	50
Snare Drum	50
Tambourine	50
Vibrating Instruments	50
Cymbals	50
Glockenspiel	51
Celesta	51
Chimes (Bells)	51
Tam-tam (Gong)	51
Triangle	52
Castanets	52
Wood Block and Cow Bell	53
Ratchet	53
Keyboard Instruments	53
Xylophone	53
Marimba	54
Vibraphone	54
Piano	54
4. THE LANGUAGE OF ORCHESTRAL MUSIC	**57**
RHYTHM	57
MELODY	58
HARMONY	59
TEXTURE	59
OTHER MUSCIAL ELEMENTS	60
SUMMARY	61

5. MAJOR FORMS OF COMPOSITION FOR THE
SYMPHONY ORCHESTRA   **63**
   SINGLE MOVEMENT COMPOSITIONS   63
      Overture   63
      Symphonic Poem   64
   MULTI-MOVEMENT COMPOSITIONS   64
      Suite   64
      Concerto   66
      Symphony   67
   INDIVIDUAL MOVEMENT FORMS   68
      Theme and Variations   68
      Rondo Form   69
      Sonata Form   69
      Forms Built Over The Bass Line   70
      Free Forms   70

6. WHAT YOU LEARN FROM A CONCERT PROGRAM   **73**
   THE CONCERT PROGRAM   73
   GLOSSARY OF TERMS   75
   FORMS AS TITLES OF MOVEMENTS   82

7. MAJOR ORCHESTRAL COMPOSERS—
THEIR LIVES AND WORKS   **85**
   BACH, J.S.   85
   BARBER   86
   BARTOK   86
   BEETHOVEN   87
   BERG   88
   BERLIOZ   89
   BERNSTEIN   90
   BIZET   90
   BRAHMS   90
   BRITTEN   91
   BRUCKNER   91
   CHOPIN   94
   COPLAND   94
   DEBUSSY   96
   DELIUS   98
   DVORAK   98
   ELGAR   99

FRANCK   99
GERSHWIN   100
GRIEG   100
HANDEL   102
HAYDN   103
HINDEMITH   103
HOLST   104
IVES   105
LISZT   106
MAHLER   106
MENDELSSOHN   107
MOZART   108
MUSSORGSKY   109
PENDERECKI   109
PROKOFIEV   110
RACHMANINOV   112
RAVEL   112
RIMSKY-KORSAKOV   113
SAINT-SAENS   114
SCHOENBERG   115
SCHUBERT   116
SCHUMANN   117
SCRIABIN   118
SHOSTAKOVICH   119
SIBELIUS   120
SMETANA   120
STRAUSS, JOHANN, JR.   121
STRAUSS, RICHARD   122
STRAVINSKY   122
TCHAIKOVSKY   124
VAUGHAN WILLIAMS   125
VIVALDI   126
WAGNER   128
WEBERN   129

8. NOW WHO'S AFRAID OF THE SYMPHONY ORCHESTRA? 131
    A BASIC REPERTOIRE LIST   132
    SUGGESTIONS FOR FURTHER READING   140
        Biographical Bibliography   140
        General Bibliography   142
    CONCERT ETIQUETTE   145

PREFACE

What does the word "Philharmonic" mean?...Why is the orchestra different in size at different times?...How often, and for how long, does the entire orchestra rehearse?...How does one train to be a conductor?...Why is rosin used on the bow hair by string instrumentalists?...What is included in a master contract of a major symphony orchestra?

Most people who attend symphony orchestra concerts—whether they are regular concertgoers, go only occasionally, or are attending a concert for the first time—ask themselves such questions. Sometimes they never find out the answers. The goal of this book is to give the audience a better understanding of the symphony orchestra and its music.

British conductor James Judd eloquently states that "music is not elitist. Such thinking betrays a total misconception about music and the arts. There are deeper things, a spiritual side to life; that is what the arts are all about. We have to encourage that if society is going to get better."

The authors sincerely hope that reading this book and referring to it often will enhance the concertgoer's understanding and enjoyment of this great institution—the symphony orchestra. However, the music itself, *"the sound of music,"* is most important. So, wherever you live, enjoy listening and support *your* symphony orchestra.

Lucas Drew
Raymond Barr

FÜNFTE SYMPHONIE

von

L. van BEETHOVEN.

Dem Fürsten von Lobkowitz und dem Grafen Rasoumoffsky gewidmet.

Op. 67.

EDWIN F. KALMUS & CO., INC.
Publishers of Music

Chapter 1

95 QUESTIONS YOU ALWAYS WANTED TO ASK ABOUT THE SYMPHONY ORCHESTRA

ABOUT THE CONCERT AND THE ORCHESTRA

1. WHAT IS A CONCERT?
A *concert* is a performance of musical compositions that does not require scenic representation. In modern history, concerts open to the general public date from around 1672 in London under the direction of the English violinist and composer John Bannister (1630-79). Franz Liszt first used the term *recital* about 1840.

2. WHAT DOES THE WORD "PHILHARMONIC" MEAN?
Literally, "philharmonic" means love (phil) of harmony.
The words *symphony orchestra* and *philharmonic orchestra* are used interchangeably as orchestral names.

3. IS IT UNUSUAL FOR WORKS FROM DIFFERENT PERIODS TO BE PERFORMED ON THE SAME CONCERT?
Program planning is the primary concern of the music director/conductor (see question #40). A good balance of musical styles is a priority in program building. However, for special purposes programs may include works of:
   a) one composer only
   b) composers of one nationality only (i.e. an all-Italian program)
   c) contemporary music only
   d) compositions centered around only a certain theme or period, etc.

4. HOW MUCH TIME DOES A GUEST SOLOIST SPEND REHEARSING WITH AN ORCHESTRA?
A guest artist usually has one or two rehearsals with the orchestra prior to a performance. However, each artist has spent a lifetime

learning—and keeping fresh—the repertoire he must have at his command.

5. DO THE LEADERS OF EACH SECTION, THE PRINCIPALS, HAVE A SAY IN THE WAY THEIR SECTIONS PERFORM?

The conductor has the overall responsibility for the interpretation of the music. The *principal player* of each section is quick to grasp the wishes of the conductor and transfer the nuances and articulations indicated by the conductor to his performance. The principal player will also mark certain indications—bowings, articulations, and the like—into his part, which the other members of his section are expected to copy into their parts. Most communication of musical ideas is non-verbal. Each musician is sensitive to the conductor's gestures, and through experience develops an acute sense of musical style.

6. ARE THE PLAYERS SITTING CLOSE TO THE CONDUCTOR BETTER MUSICIANS?

Each person in the wind and percussion sections has a separate part to play. All first violins usually play the same music, as do the second violins, violas, cellos, and double basses, respectively. The principal players have already been discussed. Associate or assistant principals are ready to lead the section if the principal player is ill, or on leave. The other members of each string section are referred to as *section players*. Traditionally, those who sit closer to the conductor and/or principal player are placed there because of ability, experience, and seniority. However, some orchestras now have a rotation policy among the section players so that instrumentalists at the rear of the section have an opportunity to sit in other places. When an opening for a section position occurs, a few major orchestras now advertise a definite place in the section (e.g., 1st Violin Section, 3rd Stand Inside Chair).

7. WHEN A CHORUS SINGS WITH AN ORCHESTRA, ARE THE MEMBERS PAID FOR THEIR SERVICES?

This will vary among choruses. In many cases the choral organization may receive a fee or honorarium and individuals sing without remuneration. In other cases an honorarium is given to each member of the chorus. Soloists are usually "imported" for major choral works. They are paid a fee similar to that received by guest instrumental soloists.

8. IN A CONCERTO, WHO LEADS—THE SOLOIST OR THE
CONDUCTOR?

A concerto is a continuous interplay between soloist and orchestra. However, the conductor and orchestra follow the soloist and all aspects of the soloist's interpretation. *Tutti* orchestra sections are those in which the whole orchestra plays without the soloist, alternating with *solo* sections, when the orchestra accompanies the soloist or the soloist plays alone.

9. WHO CHOOSES THE SIZE OF THE ORCHESTRA?

The music, thus the composer, determines the exact number of instruments in the wind and percussion section. A full symphony orchestra of 85 to 90 or more members (approximately 32 violins, 12 violas, 12 cellos, 9 basses in the string section) is required to obtain the rich string sound necessary to balance the larger wind sections.

10. CAN SMALL ORCHESTRAS PLAY MUSIC WRITTEN FOR MANY
INSTRUMENTS?

When an orchestra of 60-65 musicians plays a Tchaikovsky or Mahler symphony, the relatively larger wind sections will overbalance the strings. Likewise, Mozart's or Haydn's music, which uses relatively fewer winds, is just as likely to sound unbalanced when played by a full string section as used in a late nineteenth century or post-romantic symphony.

11. WHY IS THE ORCHESTRA DIFFERENT IN SIZE AT DIFFERENT
TIMES?

In Chapter 2, the development of the orchestra is discussed. The size of the orchestra depends on the music being played. For example, Mozart's *Symphony No. 29 in A Major K. 201* (eighteenth century) is scored for two oboes, two horns, and strings. Tchaikovsky's *Symphony No. 4* (nineteenth century) calls for strings, 3 flutes, 2 oboes, 2 clarinets, 2 bassoons, 4 horns, 2 trumpets, 3 trombones, tuba, and percussion.

12. HOW LONG ARE TYPICAL ORCHESTRAL PIECES—
SYMPHONIES, FOR EXAMPLE?

The average symphony of the Classical period lasts approximately half an hour (although Beethoven's *Choral* Symphony No. 9 lasts 65-75 minutes). The duration of most nineteenth century symphonies is from 30 to 50 minutes.

13. DO ORCHESTRAS ALWAYS PLAY A PIECE THE WAY THE COMPOSER WROTE IT?

The orchestra plays the notes, dynamics, rhythms, and articulations in the printed music as the composer indicated. The identical instruments listed in the score by the composer are used, otherwise one would not hear the timbre and orchestration intended by the composer. However, the conductor influences the musical interpretation of the composer's ideas as do certain conventions of notation.

14. ARE INSTRUMENTS AVAILABLE TODAY BUT PERHAPS NOT AT THE TIME OF COMPOSITION EVER USED?

Instruments invented or added to the orchestra since the work was written are not usually used, although in a few instances the parts written for now-obsolete instruments are taken by other, modern replacements. Parts originally written for the ophicleide, for example, are now played by the tuba. Basically, each composer has his own "sound" within the historical context of the time he lived.

15. HOW IS THE TEMPO INDICATED IN THE MUSIC? (HOW DO THEY KNOW HOW FAST TO PLAY?)

The tempo (how fast) is printed in the music (in each player's part as well as in the conductor's score). Sometimes the tempo marking might be *Allegro*, meaning quickly. Other times markings are more specific: *Allegro* (♩ = 120 beats per minute). A conductor interprets these markings and keeps everyone together.

16. HOW ARE DYNAMICS INDICATED IN THE MUSIC?

Musicians have learned a vocabulary that indicates dynamics. The table below gives an idea of the range of dynamics (how loud or soft) with their abbreviations as used in the music:

very loud	*fortissimo*	*ff*
loud	*forte*	*f*
medium loud	*mezzo-forte*	*mf*
medium soft	*mezzo-piano*	*mp*
soft	*piano*	*p*
very soft	*pianissimo*	*pp*

17. WHO CONTROLS THE TEMPO AND DYNAMICS IN THE
    ORCHESTRA?
The conductor has the overall responsibility of setting the tempo
and balancing the dynamics within the orchestra. He must listen and
control these aspects of the music as part of his interpretation.

18. WHAT DOES "OPUS" MEAN?
Opus is Latin for "work." Opus numbers identify the chronological
order of the composition and/or the publication of a composer's
works (Opus 1, Opus 2, etc.). If an *Opus* comprises more than one
work, a sub-division is often used (Opus 18, No. 2).

19. WHAT IS MEANT BY "BOWINGS"?
Bowings for stringed instruments refer to direction of the bow as
follows:

   1) "Pull" the bow = *down-bow*
   2) "Push" the bow = *up-bow*

The symbol for down-bow is ⊓, for up-bow V. The players mark
these symbols above selected notes as a reminder of the bow direction. Bow direction emphasizes the meter, phrasing, and style of the
music. Generally, the down-bow has a little more weight. Bow direction is the responsibility of the concertmaster and the section
leaders. Some conductors bow all the string parts to save time and to
ensure the coordination of the interpretation.

20. WHY ARE SECTIONS OF INSTRUMENTS PLACED IN SPECIFIC
    AREAS ON A STAGE?
Several generally accepted seating arrangements for symphony
orchestras are used. (See the diagram in Chapter 2.) Possibly the
only certain placement is that of the first violins—always in front and
on the conductor's left. The placement of the other strings may vary.
   The wind and percussion instruments are behind the strings. The
woodwinds are closer to the strings for the purpose of balance, while
the brass and percussion are placed to the rear, since they have po-
tentially more volume.

21. HOW LONG DOES IT TAKE FOR AN ORCHESTRA TO MASTER A PIECE?

Most compositions have been played previously by the musicians in a professional orchestra. Therefore, musicians bring a musical knowledge of the work and the necessary technical skill to the first rehearsal. On a typical program three works will be performed. A major orchestra that plays together nine or ten months of the year develops a sizeable repertoire of the *standard orchestral literature*, compared to an orchestra that performs one program a month and rehearses only four or five times each month. In general, twentieth century compositions may require more rehearsal. Three to five rehearsals for each concert usually allow adequate rehearsal time.

22. HOW OFTEN, AND FOR HOW LONG, DOES THE ENTIRE ORCHESTRA REHEARSE?

Major orchestras rehearse daily with usually one day off each week. Seven or eight *services* (a service equals one rehearsal or one concert) are scheduled per week. Regional and metropolitan orchestras are generally not full-time, however, and rehearsal schedules may be less regular. Three to five rehearsals of 2½ to 3 hours each are usually scheduled for each subscription concert or program. This doesn't include individual practice time.

23. DOES THE ORCHESTRA EVER REHEARSE IN SMALL GROUPS?

Many orchestras periodically divide the ensemble into sections for rehearsal. For example, the strings may rehearse alone for part of a rehearsal and then the winds (woodwind and brass) and percussion may be added. Sometimes a full rehearsal is devoted to either the strings or the winds or the brass and percussion. Coordinating articulations is one of the helpful results of this type of sectional rehearsal.

24. DOES AN ORCHESTRA "WARM UP" BEFORE A CONCERT?

An orchestra warms up individually, unlike the chorus which usually vocalizes as an ensemble, prior to a concert. Orchestra members arrive at least one half hour prior to concert time, and warm up backstage and/or on stage. They play scales and exercises, as well as review selected passages from the music to be performed. Sometimes, especially among the winds, a small group or section may discreetly practice a certain passage on stage prior to the performance.

25. HOW DOES THE ORCHESTRA TUNE?

The orchestra tunes to the note "A" (440 vibrations per second is the frequency most often used) which is played by the oboe just before the first work on the program is performed.

26. WHO TURNS THE PAGES OF THE MUSIC DURING THE PERFORMANCE?

The "inside" person on each stand (desk) in the string section usually has the responsibility of turning the page, thus allowing the "outside" players to play without interruption. Since wind players are most often playing *solo* parts, their music is edited to allow time to turn the page. Also, they do not usually play as continuously as string players.

27. HOW DOES EACH GROUP OF INSTRUMENTS KNOW WHAT THE OTHER GROUPS ARE PLAYING?

Musicians understand "the language of music," and are generally well trained in reading music, listening carefully, and watching the conductor. Order is brought to music by the meter of the composition.

28. CAN A PLAYER HEAR THE ENTIRE ORCHESTRA?

Yes, but there are many variances of balance depending on where one sits in the orchestra.

29. ARE INSTRUMENTS PLAYED "OFF-STAGE" AT TIMES?

Yes. Three well-known examples are:

Beethoven—*Leonore* Overture No. 3 (trumpet)
Berlioz—*Fantastic Symphony* (oboe)
Respighi—*The Pines of Rome* (trumpet)

30. WHY DOES THE CONCERT MASTER MAKE A SOLO ENTRANCE JUST BEFORE THE CONDUCTOR?

The concertmaster's entrance signals that the concert is about to begin. He supervises the tuning of the orchestra at the beginning and during the concert. The orchestra follows his lead when standing to acknowledge applause at the conclusion of a composition.

31. WHAT IS THE ORIGIN OF CONCERT DRESS?

White tie and tails are simply nineteenth century formal attire, still used by most major symphony orchestras. Women usually wear long black dresses, although dress pants have become acceptable in many orchestras.

32. WHAT IS THE COST OF A PIECE OF MUSIC FOR THE ENTIRE ORCHESTRA?

In order for the orchestra to perform a piece of music, a complete set of performance material must be acquired for the orchestra's use. This set of performance material will include one copy of the appropriate part for each member of the orchestra, and its cost will depend on the size of the orchestration and the particular composition. A public domain work—meaning that it is of a prescribed age and 'no royalties need be paid on it—such as Beethoven's *Symphony No. 5* may be purchased at present for about $75 to $100. A large twentieth century composition, however, may cost from $300 to $500, and most twentieth century music is available only on a rental basis.

33. WHAT HAPPENS IF A STRING BREAKS DURING A PERFORMANCE?

First, a performer tries to play the same notes on another string and change strings at the end of the movement or work.

34. ARE MISTAKES FREQUENTLY MADE IN A CONCERT?

Hopefully not! Occasionally, there may be a missed note that is obvious. However, less noticeable are minor problems of intonation and ensemble. Considering the statistical probability of things that could go wrong during a performance, most performances have an extremely high percentage of success. Orchestra members do strive for perfection. Performing in a symphony orchestra requires the utmost concentration, skill, and discipline.

THE CONDUCTOR

35. HOW DOES ONE TRAIN TO BE A CONDUCTOR?

Generally, a conductor begins his career with the study of some other aspect of orchestral performance—frequently the performance study of one or more of the orchestral instruments. A thorough knowledge of all aspects of the orchestra is essential, as well as an understanding of musical form. Many conductors find it especially helpful to have a particularly detailed understanding of the strings of the orchestra. Some ability as a pianist is also helpful for study purposes.

36. WHO CHOOSES THE CONDUCTOR?

In the U.S.A. the conductor and/or music director is selected by the board of directors of each symphony orchestra. The musicians in some instances may have the opportunity to recommend or evaluate conductorial candidates, but their recommendations are only advisory. The board, as the employer, engages the conductor and negotiates his contract. Each orchestra will have its own variations on this basic progression of events.

37. HOW DOES THE CONDUCTOR KNOW WHICH INSTRUMENT SHOULD PLAY AND WHEN?

The conductor has everyone's music in front of him. This is called the *score* and contains the music of all the instruments.

38. MUST A CONDUCTOR ALWAYS USE A SCORE?

A conductor may or may not use a score in performance. However, he must know the score thoroughly, whether or not he has it before him, otherwise the performance suffers.

39. WHY WOULD A CONDUCTOR CONDUCT WITHOUT A SCORE?

Many conductors prefer to conduct from memory to have greater freedom of movement and expression. Turning pages during a performance can also interrupt the flow of conducting. We must emphasize that a conductor must know his score thoroughly, regardless of whether he chooses to have it before him during the performance.

40. WHO DECIDES WHAT MUSIC THE ORCHESTRA SHOULD PLAY FOR ANY GIVEN CONCERT?

In the U.S.A. the music director and/or conductor plans the repertoire. He also supervises the overall programming of guest and assistant conductors. He strives for a balance of literature from different periods, as well as, hopefully, being creative and innovative in program selection.

41. WHO CHOOSES THE SOLO PERFORMERS FOR CONCERTOS?

The conductor and/or music director, in consultation with the management of the orchestra, engages the soloists. Sometimes a principal player of the orchestra is invited to play a concerto.

42. IS THERE A FORMAT TO THE WAVING THE CONDUCTOR'S HANDS ARE DOING?

The right hand of the conductor is used mainly for beating patterns that indicate the meter of the music. The beat sets a tempo for the music. The left hand may be used to indicate dynamics (loud, soft, crescendo, diminuendo, etc.) The eyes and other motions of the body also convey the character of the music.

43. WHAT ARE THE PATTERNS THE CONDUCTOR SEEMS TO FOLLOW?

The main motions the conductor makes are to indicate the meter of the music as shown below:

Two Beats   *Three Beats*   *Four Beats*

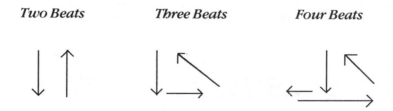

44. COULD AN ORCHESTRA PLAY WITHOUT A CONDUCTOR?

Yes. However, it would be much more difficult to play nineteenth and twentieth century music than the seventeenth and eighteenth century repertoire without a conductor. Some twentieth century music would fall into the "practically impossible" category without a conductor.

45. WHO TAKES OVER SHOULD THE CONDUCTOR BECOME ILL OR SUDDENLY UNAVAILABLE?

An orchestra usually has an assistant or associate conductor who would assist in an emergency.

47. HAS ANY CONDUCTOR PERFORMED AS SOLOIST IN A CONCERTO?

Yes. It is not uncommon to have a "pianist/conductor" both perform and conduct a concerto. Two well-known musicians who do this are Leonard Bernstein and André Previn.

47. WHEN REHEARSING FOR A PERFORMANCE DOES THE DIRECTOR OF THE CHORUS HAVE A PART IN CONDUCTING HIS SINGERS?

The choral director conducts and prepares the chorus at appropriate rehearsals prior to rehearsing with the orchestra. When the rehearsals with the orchestra begin, the conductor of the symphony orchestra usually conducts the rehearsals and concert.

48. HOW DOES THE CONDUCTOR ACKNOWLEDGE APPLAUSE?

The conductor bows and the orchestra stands to acknowledge the applause of the audience. This process recurs as long as the response is enthusiastic.

49. WHAT IF THE CONDUCTOR SHOULD DROP THE BATON?

Usually, there is an extra baton on the conductor's stand or on the stand of one of the instrumentalists close to the conductor; otherwise he continues to conduct without the baton. Leopold Stokowski is one conductor who developed an expressive style of conducting without a baton.

50. WHAT EFFECT DOES A CHANGE IN CONDUCTORS HAVE ON THE MUSICIANS?

Each conductor will have his own way of communicating, both verbally and non-verbally, with an orchestra. An orchestra will make its adjustments to a guest conductor quickly during the first rehearsal, if he is an excellent one. In many year-round orchestras, the principal conductor may conduct only 12 to 16 weeks annually. Many guest conductors come before an orchestra during the year. This is the age of the "jet set" conductor!

51. ARE CONDUCTORS ALSO COMPOSERS, AND HOW DOES ONE TRAIN TO BE A COMPOSER?

Conductors are frequently composers, and sometimes it is only chance circumstances that will cause a composer to become known mainly as a conductor, or vice versa. This is the case partly because a composer's training is essentially the same as a conductor's—a thorough schooling in all aspects of instrumentation, music history and form. Some will choose to use their training in the essentially recreative role of conductor, while others will feel compelled to create their own, new music. Some artists have a combined career as a performer/conductor, composer/conductor, performer/composer or different aspects of all three careers.

ILLUSTRATION BY MATTHEW GANNON

ORCHESTRAL MUSICIANS AND THEIR INSTRUMENTS

52. HOW OLD ARE MOST MUSICIANS WHEN THEY BEGIN TO PLAY AN INSTRUMENT FOR THE FIRST TIME?

In many communities, children have the opportunity to begin the study of string, wind and percussion instruments in elementary school (fourth or fifth grade at approximately 10 years of age). One might wait until later for certain larger instruments. Some violinists begin with the Suzuki approach during pre-school years. Piano lessons at an early age provide an excellent background for any orchestral instrumentalist. Wind instrument training usually is begun a little later, as it requires somewhat greater maturity of lips, lungs, and facial muscles.

53. DO MOST ORCHESTRAL MUSICIANS KNOW HOW TO PLAY MORE THAN ONE INSTRUMENT?

Most have a background of piano as a secondary instrument. However, the majority of symphony orchestra musicians concentrate on one instrument. The exceptions are percussionists and woodwind players, who play more than one instrument.

54. HOW MANY HOURS A DAY DOES EACH ORCHESTRAL MUSICIAN PRACTICE?

Most professional musicians have been practicing and developing their skills from an early age. Generally several hours (two to four) of individual practice per day will maintain and improve one's technique. Additional time may be required when learning new repertoire. This is in addition to orchestra rehearsals and performances. Practicing is a lifelong job!

55. WHY DO STRING PLAYERS SOMETIMES PUT DOWN THEIR BOWS AND PLAY THEIR INSTRUMENTS WITH THEIR FINGERS?

A string player may pluck the string with the finger(s) of the right hand, with or without holding the bow. This is called *pizzicato*. Most often the bow is held when playing *pizzicato* so it is easier to return quickly to bowing. The term *arco* appears in the music to signal the use of the bow after playing *pizzicato*. However, when the entire movement of a symphony is *pizzicato* (for example, the third movement of Tchaikovsky's *Symphony No. 4*), the string instrumentalists usually put down their bows.

56. DO PERCUSSION PLAYERS KNOW HOW TO PLAY ALL PERCUSSION INSTRUMENTS?

Generally, percussionists are skilled as performers on all percussion instruments

57. DOES IT REALLY TAKE VERY MUCH SKILL TO HIT A GONG OR CYMBAL JUST RIGHT?

Anyone can "hit" a gong, cymbal or drum, but to strike it at the precise moment, with the required sensitivity, takes musicianship and skill. Further, tuning the timpani requires a well-trained ear.

58. WHY IS THERE NOT ONE PERFORMER FOR EACH PERCUSSION INSTRUMENT?

Very often parts are not played simultaneously and there is ample time to move between instruments, so one player can perform several parts in a composition. For example, the bass drum, cymbals, and triangle may be played by the same person.

59. WHY DO SOME REED PLAYERS OFTEN KEEP THEIR REEDS IN THEIR MOUTHS?

Oboists and bassoonists must keep their reeds moist during the performance while they are "resting" or not playing. A reed that is wet will vibrate properly, producing a good tone.

60. WHY DOES A BASSOONIST KEEP BLOWING AIR THROUGH HIS BASSOON WHILE NOT PLAYING?

Keeping the reed moist was discussed in question #59. Similarly, wind players may keep the instrument "warm" by lightly breathing air through the instrument while waiting to play.

61. DOES A PIANO SOLOIST HAVE A HARD TIME ADJUSTING TO DIFFERENT PIANOS?

Yes, because the "touch" of a piano is unique. For this reason, an important aspect of being a concert pianist is the ability to adjust to different instruments. Most artists prefer a piano from one of the top three or four makers of concert grand pianos. If they are unable to have the same piano from one engagement to the next, at least they can become accustomed to the characteristics of the instruments of one manufacturer.

62. DOES THE PIANO SOLOIST BRING HIS OWN PIANO?

Rarely does a pianist perform on his own piano. The piano is either owned or rented by the local orchestra.

63. SOME OF THE PLAYERS MOVE AROUND A LOT WHILE PERFORMING. DOES THIS AFFECT THEIR PLAYING?

Just as conductors have different gestures for various musical styles, so do instrumentalists. Instrumentalists should move freely, for the instrument is an extension of the body. However, excessive movements may be distracting and may not be productive technically for the performer.

64. WHAT IS THE PREREQUISITE FOR BEING A FIRST VIOLINIST?

In general, the first violin part is frequently more demanding and involves a higher range than the second violin music. However, this does not mean that a second violinist could not play first violin; he just has to win the audition, if a position is open in the section.

65. WHY IS ROSIN USED ON THE BOW HAIR BY STRING INSTRUMENTALISTS?

Rosin is applied to the hair of the bows by all string players. The rosin used respectively for the violin, viola, cello and double bass is slightly different in composition. The sticky substance aids the fibers of the bow hair to "grip" the string, thus setting the string in vibration.

66. WHY DO THE VIOLINS, VIOLAS AND OTHER BOWED STRINGED INSTRUMENTS MOVE THEIR BOWS IN THE SAME DIRECTION AT THE SAME TIME?

Often two or more sections play an identical passage. By using the same bow direction they achieve a similar phrasing and sound (refer to question 19)

67. HOW OFTEN DOES A MUSICIAN PURCHASE AN INSTRUMENT OR DOES HE KEEP ONE FOR HIS ENTIRE LIFE?

A general answer is very difficult to give. By the time a musician has become a member of a professional orchestra, he is probably not still using the first instrument on which he began his study. Usually a symphony musician owns several instruments, preferring one of them for orchestral use. Sometimes the orchestra will provide an instrument. Most players are always looking for a better or "perfect" instrument throughout their careers. The older string instruments are a good investment and continue to increase in value. Wind instrumentalists generally use newer instruments.

68. HOW MUCH DOES EACH INSTRUMENT COST?

New wind and percussion instruments are usually preferred and are not as expensive as professional-level stringed instruments. Some very good new stringed instruments are available, but most string players play older and usually more valuable instruments. A very good wind instrument might be in the price range of a minimum level string instrument ($5,000 to $15,000). Fine string instruments increase in value and one would expect to pay tens of thousands of dollars. Some violins are valued at more than $100,000.

69. IS THE HARPSICHORD USED TODAY?

The harpsichord has enjoyed an entirely appropriate reacceptance into concert life, in recognition of the fact that it was the dominant keyboard instrument throughout most of the eighteenth century. Its use is appropriate in many eighteenth century orchestral works, and it is also featured in a number of twentieth century works including the *Petite Symphonie Concertante* (1944-45) by Frank Martin.

70. IS THERE ANY "HIERARCHY" WITHIN EACH GROUP OF INSTRUMENTS?

The principal player is the leader of a particular section of instruments. The string principals in consultation with the concertmaster set bowings for their respective sections, and occasionally play short solo passages; the wind principals have solo melodic parts periodically and set articulations within their sections. The principal percussionist organizes the many parts and instruments in the percussion section (i.e., snare drum, cymbals, triangle, xylophone, etc.).

71. WHY DO PERFORMERS SOMETIMES PUT GADGETS ON, OR INTO, THEIR INSTRUMENTS DURING THE PERFORMANCE?

The "gadgets" are *mutes*. The mute is placed on the bridge of a stringed instrument to give it a softer sound and to alter the tone color. Brass instrumentalists place a mute in the bell of the instrument. The horn player also mutes his instrument by placing his right hand in the bell. Mutes are rarely used on flutes, oboes, clarinets, or bassoons.

72. WHY DOES THE TIMPANIST LISTEN TO HIS DRUMS WHEN HE IS NOT PLAYING THEM?

When a timpanist places his ear close to the drum head during a performance, he is checking the tuning of the drum. In early symphonies, the timpanist played relatively few notes per movement, generally only two, one on each drum. However, since Beethoven and especially since the invention of the timpani pedal-tuning device, the player may be asked to play several different notes during a piece, and this will require discreet re-tuning of one or more drums while the piece is in progress.

73. WHAT IS AN "ONDES MARTENOT"?

The *ondes martenot* is an electronic keyboard instrument patented in 1922 by its French inventor, Maurice Martenot. It is used in Olivier Messiaen's *Turangalila Symphony for Solo Piano and Orchestra* (1948).

74. ARE THERE VIOLINS OF DIFFERENT PITCHES?

All violins are tuned to the same pitches. However, the violin section is divided into two parts. The first violins most often play the melody line of the music while the second violins generally play an accompanying or harmony part. Often they accompany the first violins. These are the traditional roles of each section. Second violin parts in contemporary music, however, can be of equal importance and difficulty.

75. WHY DO SOME BASS PLAYERS SEEM TO HOLD THEIR BOWS DIFFERENTLY FROM OTHER BASS PLAYERS?

Two types of double bass bows are in use. The French bow is the one similar in shape to the cello bow, only slightly larger. The German double bass bow is shaped and held differently. It is derived from the older viola da gamba style of bowing.

76. WHY DO SOME OF THE DOUBLE BASSES HAVE AN EXTENDED PIECE ON THE TOP?

Some double basses have an extended fingerboard for the lowest string to produce (with the aid of a mechanical device) several lower notes. These additional lower notes are not possible without such an extension or a fifth string.

THE ORGANIZATION AND ROUTINE
OF A SYMPHONY ORCHESTRA

77. WHO SPONSORS AN ORCHESTRA?
In the U.S.A. an orchestra is usually a chartered non-profit organization governed by a board of directors.

78. HOW ARE ORCHESTRAS PRESENTLY CLASSIFIED BY THE AMERICAN SYMPHONY ORCHESTRA LEAGUE?
Orchestras are classified according to budget.

79. WHAT IS THE MUSICIANS' UNION?
The Musicians' Union (American Federation of Musicians—AFM) is a national labor organization that sets minimum standards for wages and working conditions. Practically all symphonic musicians belong to this union. Each city has its own local chapter of the American Federation of Musicians to set local policies.

80. WHAT IS THE FUNCTION OF THE ORCHESTRA COMMITTEE?
The Orchestra Committee represents the musicians in negotiations with the symphony orchestra management and the Musician's Union. The committee is elected by the members of the orchestra.

81. WHAT IS INCLUDED IN A MASTER CONTRACT OF A MAJOR SYMPHONY ORCHESTRA?
The master contract or agreement for a major symphony orchestra is between the orchestra and the local chapter of the American Federation of Musicians. The following is a list of some of the areas addressed in a typical contract.
1. Definitions and Operating Principles.
2. Concert Season(s) Covered by the Agreement.
3. Compensation: Wages, Health Insurance, Pension, Instrument Insurance, etc.
4. Tours and Runouts (Travel Conditions).
5. Number and Type(s) of Services.
6. Notices and Schedule Conditions.
7. Absences, Leaves, etc.
8. Special Covenants of the Musician.
9. Employment of Musicians, Probationary Period, Dismissal, Review Procedures, etc.

10. Vacancies.
11. Audition Procedures.
12. Instrumentation of Orchestra and Duties of Specific Personnel.
13. Contract Legality and Duration.

82. WHAT IS THE DURATION OF THE CONTRACT BETWEEN THE ORCHESTRA AND ITS MUSICIANS?

The usual labor contract between the musicians and the management of the orchestra (board of directors) is from one to three years.

83. WHAT ARE THE DUTIES OF THE PERSONNEL MANAGER?

Some of the duties of the personnel manager include the following:

1. Be the official representative of the orchestra at all services and keep the members of the orchestra informed.
2. Be responsible for keeping time at all services and for all travel arrangements.
3. Hire extra and substitute musicians.
4. List all absences from services, all tardiness and reasons for such absences and tardiness.
5. Be responsible for the monitoring of concert dress.

84. WHAT ARE THE DUTIES OF THE LIBRARIAN?

Some of the duties of the librarian include the following:

1. Responsibility for cataloging the music library of the symphony orchestra.
2. Responsibility for ordering music either to purchase or to rent.
3. Responsibility for securing music on time for parts to be distributed to musicians, usually two weeks before the first rehearsal of such music.
4. Responsibility for returning the music to the library or to the publisher.
5. Responsibility for supplying the conductor with a score and for seeing that all parts are properly placed on the music stands prior to a rehearsal or a performance.
6. Responsibility for entering all corrections, bowings, and other modifications into the parts.

85. HOW DO PEOPLE GO ABOUT GETTING INTO A SYMPHONY ORCHESTRA?

Auditions are held periodically as openings occur. The applicant usually plays excerpts from the solo repertoire of his instrument and excerpts from the orchestral literature.

86. WHO CHOOSES THE MUSICIANS IN THE ORCHESTRA?

To enter the orchestra, musicians audition for the conductor and a committee of musicians selected from the orchestra, with the final decision made by the music director.

87. WHO DECIDES IF A MUSICIAN IS NOT PLAYING AS WELL AS HE SHOULD BE?

In most ensembles the first year or two are probationary. The music director has the responsibility to dismiss or award non-probationary status to each musician at the end of this period. Non-probationary musicians may be dismissed if their musicianship and skills are not maintained. A procedure for dismissal as well as for the review of the decision is part of the master contract of each symphony orchestra.

MISCELLANEOUS

88. WHAT IS A "POPS" ORCHESTRA?

Pops is short for popular. Pops concerts usually feature well-known classical compositions as well as music from the theater, films, jazz, rock, etc. Pops refers to music generally familiar to the broadest audiences.

89. DO ORCHESTRAS PERFORM FILM MUSIC AT CONCERTS?

Recent film music is more often performed at "Pops" Concerts. Aaron Copland wrote the music for the film *The Red Pony* and Leonard Bernstein composed the score for *On the Waterfront*. John Williams's music to *Star Wars* is quite popular.

90. IS MUSIC WRITTEN FOR ACCORDION AND ORCHESTRA?

Gordon Jacob, the twentieth century English composer, has written a *Concerto for Accordion and Orchestra*. Sometimes pops concerts feature instruments such as the harmonica, glass harmonica, musical saw, etc.

91. IS THE PIANO SOMETIMES USED AS AN ORCHESTRAL INSTRUMENT?

Yes, the music of Stravinsky, Copland, and Shostakovich, among other composers, often employs the piano as an orchestral instrument.

92. WHAT IS A CHAMBER ORCHESTRA?

In general, a chamber orchestra is a small symphony orchestra with 20 to 40 instrumentalists. The foundation of its repertoire is in the Baroque and Classical periods.

93. ARE EXTRA-MUSICAL SOUNDS EVER USED IN A SYMPHONIC WORK?

In Respighi's *Pines of Rome* a phonograph recording (now on tape) of a nightingale is used at the end of the third movement. It is "played" by a percussionist.

94. IS MUSIC WRITTEN FOR ORCHESTRA AND NARRATOR?

Yes, Copland's *Lincoln Portrait* for Narrator and Symphony Orchestra is well known. Prokofiev's *Peter and the Wolf* is popular at children's concerts.

95. IS THE ORGAN USED WITH SYMPHONY ORCHESTRA?

The organ is not used very often, but it has an important part in Saint-Saëns's *Symphony No. 3* and Richard Strauss's *Thus Spake Zarathustra*.

ILLUSTRATION BY MATTHEW GANNON

The Philadelphia Orchestra, Riccardo Muti, Music Director.

Chapter 2

THE DEVELOPMENT OF THE ORCHESTRA

Vocal music clearly dominated instrumental music until around 1600. Gregorian Chant (c. 600-900 A.D.) was written specifically for the church. From about 850 A.D. polyphonic music developed, reaching a high point in the works of Palestrina (c. 1515-1594). The church collected and copied its music, thus preserving it for future generations. Much of the secular music of the time was improvised and not written down—thus it has not been preserved.

During the sixteenth century, composers wrote primarily for individual instrumentalists. As problems with intonation were reduced, composers wrote more frequently for small instrumental combinations or consorts. However, large ensembles of musicians were assembled for ceremonial and festive occasions.

BAROQUE PERIOD

During the Baroque period (c. 1600-1750), instrumental music achieved an importance equal to that of vocal music. The instrumental ensemble that developed into the symphony orchestra stems from the seventeenth century with the string instruments being the core of the ensemble. Note the instrumentation of Johann Sebastian Bach's six Brandenburg Concertos, all of which include a keyboard "continuo" (usually harpsichord) in addition to the instrumentation shown:

Concerto No. 1: Strings with two horns and three oboes
No. 2: Strings with trumpet, flute, and oboe
No. 3: 3 violins, 3 violas, 3 cellos, and double bass
No. 4: Strings with two recorders and violin solo
No. 5: Strings with flute, violin solo, and harpsichord solo
No. 6: 2 violas, 2 viole da gamba, cello, and double bass

Several works from this era are quite popular at present. Antonio Vivaldi's (c.1685-1741) *The Seasons* is an early example of descrip-

23

tive music for solo violin and string orchestra. Two other baroque works—the *Water Music* and the *Royal Fireworks Music* of Handel —were written for special occasions and were first performed outdoors.

An instrumental repertoire was established during the baroque period, even though there was little standardization of instrumentation. Composers of that period wrote concerti grossi, suites, and sinfonias for a heterogeneous collection of instruments.

The composer and performer of music were dependent on the benevolence and munificence of the aristocracy, a situation referred to as patronage. Exceptions to the exclusivity of music performance in private, aristocratic circles were principally performances found in the church, but also those in the public rooms in London, and in opera theaters such as the Teatro San Cassiano in Venice.

CLASSICAL PERIOD

By the mid-eighteenth century, court orchestras flourished in Paris, Milan, Vienna, Berlin, Dresden, and Mannheim. Instrumentalists, especially at the larger centers of activity, helped to develop and inspire the composers' creative energies. The court orchestra was used to accompany voices in church services and operas, as well as accompanying instrumental soloists in concertos.

Ensembles were also beginning to perform their own emerging form — the symphony. In 1782 the famous Mannheim Orchestra boasted 18 violins, three violas, four cellos, three double basses, four flutes, three oboes, three clarinets, four bassoons, four horns, and possibly trumpets and timpani.

The instrumentation of an early and late symphony of Haydn and of Mozart, respectively, demonstrate the evolution of instrumentation in the classical period (c. 1750-1825):

	Haydn
Symphony No. 6	Strings with flute, two oboes, bassoon, two horns, and continuo
Symphony No. 104	Strings with two flutes, two oboes, two clarinets, two bassoons, two horns, two trumpets, and timpani

Mozart

Symphony No. 1   Strings with two oboes, two horns, and continuo

Symphony No. 41   Strings with flute, two oboes, two bassoons, two horns, two trumpets, and timpani

NINETEENTH CENTURY

In the late eighteenth century, music performance began to be less confined to programs for the nobility, and became more public in concert halls and concert societies. As a general trend in the nineteenth century, the court musician became the employee of the city or state. Concerts in the private chambers of royalty and the aristocracy gave way to concerts organized and sponsored by the public for its own enjoyment, marking an end to the long-standing concept of patronage.

During the latter part of the nineteenth century several concert halls still in use today were built. Among them are the Royal Albert Hall in London (1871), Carnegie Hall in New York (1891), and Symphony Hall in Boston (1899).

Famous orchestras of the period established an instrumentation maintained in twentieth century performance. Around the middle of the nineteenth century, for example, the Paris Opera had 23 violins, eight violas, ten cellos, and eight double basses.

During the early part of the nineteenth century, the practice of conducting orchestral and operatic performances with a baton began to supersede the older style of joint direction by a "conductor" seated at a keyboard instrument and the "violinist-leader" (concertmaster). Carl Maria von Weber in Dresden, Louis Spohr in Frankfurt, and Felix Mendelssohn in Leipzig were among the pioneer conductors who first used a baton during the first quarter of the century.

Spohr gives, in his autobiography, the following account of his experience of conducting the Philharmonic of London in 1820.

It was at that time still the custom that when symphonies and overtures were performed, the pianist had the score before him, not exactly to conduct from it, but only to read after and to play with the orchestra at pleasure, which, when it was heard, had a very bad effect. The real conductor was the first violin, who gave the tempi, and now and then, when the orchestra began to falter, gave the beat with the bow of his violin. So numerous an orchestra, standing so far apart from each other as that of the Philharmonic, could not possibly go exactly together, and in spite of the excellence of the individual members, the ensemble was much worse than we are accustomed to in Germany. I had, therefore, resolved when my turn came to direct, to make an attempt to remedy this defective system. Fortunately at the morning rehearsal on the day when I was to conduct the concert, Mr. Ries took the place at the piano, and he readily assented to give up the score to me and to remain wholly excluded from all participation in the [direction of the] performance. I then took my stand with the score at a separate music desk in front of the orchestra, drew my directing baton from my coat pocket and gave the signal to begin. Quite alarmed at such a novel procedure, some of the directors would have protested against it; but when I besought them to grant me at least one trial, they became pacified. The symphonies and overtures that were to be rehearsed were well known to me, and in Germany I had already directed at their performance. I therefore could not only give the tempi in a very decisive manner, but indicated also to the wind instruments and horns all their entries, which ensured to them a confidence such as hitherto they had not known there. I also took the liberty, when the execution did not satisfy me, to stop, and in a very polite but earnest manner to remark upon the manner of execution, which remarks Mr. Ries at my request interpreted to the orchestra. Incited thereby to more than usual attention, and conducted with certainty by the visible manner of giving the time, they played with a spirit and correctness such as till then they had never been heard to play with. Surprised and inspired by this result, the orchestra, immediately after the first part of the symphony, expressed aloud its collective assent to the new mode of conducting, and thereby overruled all further opposition on the part of the directors. In the vocal pieces also, the conducting of which I assumed at the request of Mr. Ries, particularly in the recitative, the leading with the baton, after I had explained the meaning of my movements, was completely successful, and the singers repeatedly expressed to me their satisfaction with the precision with which the orchestra now followed them. . . . The triumph of the baton as a time-giver was decisive, and no one was seen any more seated at the piano during the performance of symphonies and overtures.[1]

The nineteenth century also inaugurated the establishment of several important conservatories or schools of music to educate orchestral players and composers. Among such institutions founded at that time were the Paris Conservatory (1795), the Prague Conservatory (1811), the Vienna Conservatory (1821), and the Royal Academy of Music in London (1822).

TWENTIETH CENTURY

During the first half of the twentieth century, symphony orchestras were developed in practically every major city of the United States. Many new cultural centers were built during the second half of the twentieth century. The building of the Lincoln Center for the Performing Arts in New York in 1962 helped to initiate this growth of new and renovated facilities. Private foundations, such as those of Ford and Rockefeller, and government aid through the National Endowment for the Arts, and state and local arts councils, have also supported music organizations. However, donations from individuals and the local business community and ticket sales remain the main source of financial support for an orchestra.

A TYPICAL ORCHESTRAL SEATING DIAGRAM

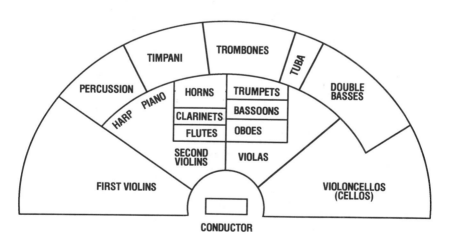

SUMMARY: EIGHTEENTH-TWENTIETH CENTURY

The evolution of string instruments has been one of numbers—from a chamber ensemble of strings during the baroque period to the twentieth century symphony orchestra of approximately 36 violins, 12 violas, 12 cellos, and nine double basses. (The number of string players is not usually indicated in the score.)

String instruments are similar today to the instruments of 300 years ago. However, many mechanical improvements to woodwind and brass instruments have been made during this time. Adam Carse states in his *History of Orchestration* that "the delicate little axle connecting the movement of two or more keys on a woodwind instrument and the ingenious valve which governs the byways in the tube of a brass instrument have been great and vitalizing gifts which have made modern orchestration possible."[2]

The evolution of instrumentation of the symphony orchestra is illustrated by the following works from the eighteenth, nineteenth, and twentieth centuries:

MOZART (1788)	*BEETHOVEN (1808)*	*MAHLER (1902)*
SYMPHONY No. 40	*SYMPHONY No. 5*	*SYMPHONY No. 5*
(First Movement)	(Fourth Movement)	(First Movement)
Strings	Strings	Strings
Flute	Piccolo	4 Flutes
2 Oboes	2 Flutes	3 Oboes
2 Clarinets	2 Oboes	3 Clarinets
2 Bassoons	2 Clarinets	2 Bassoons
2 Horns	2 Bassoons	Contrabassoon
	Contrabassoon	6 Horns
	2 Horns	4 Trumpets
	2 Trumpets	3 Trombones
	3 Trombones	Tuba
	Timpani	Percussion
		Timpani

NOTES

1. Adam Carse, *The History of Orchestration* (New York: Dover Publications, Inc., 1964.
2. *Ibid.*

Chapter 3

THE INSTRUMENTS OF THE ORCHESTRA

STRING INSTRUMENTS

The string instruments make up nearly 70% of the symphony orchestra. These instruments, with the exception of the harp, have a number of things in common. They all have four strings (the bass may have five) stretched over a hollow box, they are played either by drawing a horsehair bow over the strings or by plucking with the fingers, and they look very much alike, except for their difference in size. The string instruments of a symphony orchestra, when considered together, make up a kind of instrumental choir with, generally, the soprano and alto parts being played by the first and second violins, the tenor part being played by the violas and the bass part being played by the cellos and double basses.

Violin

The violins are frequently the melody instruments of the orchestra. The principal first violinist is called the *concertmaster*, and is sometimes also the assistant conductor of the orchestra. Usually the first violin section has 14-20 players and the second violin section 12-18 players.

The violin is an instrument which has remained relatively unchanged since its creation by the three great violin-making families of Cremona, Italy—the Stradivaris, the Amatis, and the Guarneris—some three hundred years ago.

The violin is considered to be such a personal instrument that it has been given the names of parts of the human body, such as the neck, shoulders, belly, and back. The violin is basically a hollow sounding-box over which four strings are attached. These strings are attached at the bottom of the instrument, called the *tail-piece*, then stretched over a small wooden piece called the *bridge* (which transmits the sound of the vibrating strings into the resonating chamber

29

PHOTO: BACHRACH

PHOTO: BACHRACH

Norman Carol, concertmaster, **Luis Biava, principal second vio-**
The Philadelphia Orchestra. lin, The Philadelphia Orchestra.

of the instrument itself), and at the top of the instrument, they are attached to pegs with which they are either tightened or loosened.
The tighter the strings are, the higher the pitch. Two holes in the instrument, called *sound holes* (or "f" holes), help the resonating
sound of the strings to be heard.

The violinist plays the instrument by placing it on his shoulder and
under his chin. He then touches the various strings with the fingers
of his left hand, thereby making the strings effectively shorter or
longer as his hand moves up or down the fingerboard. The shorter
the string, the higher the pitch.

The bow is a long wooden stick to which are attached numerous
strands of hair, usually taken from a horse's tail. The lower part of the
bow (called the "frog") has a mechanism which allows the violinist
to make the hair as tight as he wishes. The player prepares the bow by
drawing it over a small block of solidified rosin (tree sap), to give it
the friction it needs to make the strings vibrate when the player actu-

ally draws the bow over the strings. In melodic passages, the player subtly rocks the fingers of the left hand as they touch the strings, to give the resonating strings a fuller, richer character—a technique known as *vibrato*.

With the right hand, the violinist draws the bow over the strings to make them resonate or, occasionally, he plucks the strings with his fingers (a technique known as *pizzicato.*) Other violin techniques which may be noticed are *glissando* (sliding the finger of the left hand rapidly up or down on the string as it is bowed), *tremolo* (moving the bow rapidly up and down to create a shimmering or trembling effect), *col legno* (playing with the wood of the bow), *sul ponticello* (bowing near the bridge), and *sul tasto* (bowing near the finger board).

The strings of the violin are tuned to the pitches of G, D, A, and E, which are each a fifth apart (five notes apart on the musical scale). It is by playing these adjacent strings together that the violinist tunes his instrument, since the interval of a fifth is relatively easy for a musician to discern. He raises or lowers the pitch of each string, in the process of tuning the instrument, by tightening or loosening the pegs on the scroll of the violin. The violin has a small wooden (or rubber) device called a *mute*, which is fastened to the bridge. The mute does not silence the string, as the name implies, but merely softens it, creating a more mellow sound.

Viola

Everything that has been said about the violin is true about the *viola* (pronounced "vee-O'-la") as well, except that the viola is larger than the violin and its strings are tuned to lower pitches (C-G-D-A). Thus it produces a sound which is somewhat lower in pitch and a bit more mellow than that of the violin. The viola, like the violin, also has a mute which is used occasionally. The placement of the violas in the orchestra is usually in front of, or slightly to the right of, the conductor. About 10-16 violas are employed in the full symphony orchestra.

Violoncello (Cello)

The *violoncello*, usually referred to simply as the *cello* (pronounced "chello"), is similar to both the viola and the violin except that it is larger. It is so large, in fact, that it cannot be played by placing it under the chin, but is held between the player's knees, with the player seated, the instrument resting on the floor on a metal peg which is attached to the bottom of the cello. The highest string on

Joseph de Pasquale, principal viola, The Philadelphia Orchestra.

William Stokking, principal cello, The Philadelphia Orchestra.

Marilyn Costello, principal harp, The Philadelphia Orchestra.

Roger Scott, principal bass, The Philadelphia Orchestra.

the cello (A) is tuned just one step higher than the lowest string on the violin (G). The cello strings, from low to high, are tuned to the pitches C-G-D-A. The cello, like the violin and viola, also has a mute, which is used occasionally. There are about 10-12 cellos in the full symphony orchestra.

Double Bass

The largest instrument of the string section of the orchestra is the *double bass*, also known as the *string bass*, *contrabass*, or *bass viol*. The bass is not a larger violin, as the viola and cello are, but a descendant of the viol family, a group of string instruments which predates the violin family (the violin, viola, and cello). The most striking difference in the appearance of the bass is that the shoulders of some instruments are sloping, rather than rounded as in the case of the violin, viola, and cello. The bass is so large that the player must stand (or sit on a high stool) to play it. The instrument's strings are thicker than the strings of the violin, viola, and cello, and some basses even have a fifth string, or an extended mechanical device on the fourth string. The bass is tuned to the pitches E-A-D-G. The fifth string would be tuned to C, a third below the lowest string of the four-string bass. The two types of double bass bows are discussed in Chapter 1. The bass, like the violin, viola, and cello, has a mute which is used occasionally. There are about 8-10 basses in the full symphony orchestra.

One final note, with reference to all of the stringed instruments, pertains to their value. The cost of these stringed instruments can run into tens of thousands of dollars, especially those made by the eighteenth century Italian master craftsmen, such as Stradavari, Amati, and Guarneri. In 1979 a Guarneri del Gesù violin, for example, was sold in London for more than $350,000.

Harp

The only other string instrument which is a regular member of the symphony orchestra is the harp. The modern concert harp is a large, freestanding instrument, more than six feet tall and weighing about 80 pounds. It has 46 or 47 strings, the lowest pitch being C or D and the highest being G. So that the harpist can more easily find his or her way around the instrument, all C strings are colored red and all F strings are colored purple.

The harp has seven pedals, one for each musical pitch in its natural, flatted or sharped form (note: there are seven different notes in the scale, the eighth being similar in sound to the first). The harpist must constantly adjust these pedals according to the key of the music being played. The pedals have three positions. The middle position is used when the pitch of the strings attached to that pedal are neither flatted nor sharped in the key in question. The lower position of the pedals is used to raise the pitch of the strings, if there are sharped notes in the scale, and the upper position is used to lower the pitch, if there are flatted notes in the scale. Most keys in music (with the exception of C major and A minor) contain a varying number of flats or sharps. Since most orchestral works do not remain in the same key throughout, the harpist must constantly be adjusting the pedals to accommodate the new keys through which the music moves.

The harpist can play single notes, melodic intervals and chords, or can strum the strings in what is called a glissando, the sound most people associate with the instrument. The harp is not used in all orchestral music, as are the other string instruments, but some composers have a predilection for the instrument and use it frequently in their works.

Guitar

One of the most popular stringed instruments, the *guitar*, is not a regular member of the orchestra. A few composers, however, have used it in their works and a number of concertos have been written for the guitar.

WIND INSTRUMENTS

The wind instruments are the second major group of instruments in the symphony orchestra. Their sound is produced by causing a column of air inside the wind instruments to vibrate. The two groups of wind instruments in the orchestra are the *woodwinds* and the *brasses*.

The woodwinds are so named because originally they were all made of wood. In the case of the flutes, this is now frequently not the case, as many flutes are made of metal, some even of platinum! The three types of woodwind instruments are: 1) those in which the sound is produced by simply blowing into the instrument (such as a flute); 2) those in which a thin, flexible piece of cane, called a *reed*, is attached to a mouthpiece (such as a clarinet) and, when the reed is set in motion by blowing into the instrument, the column of air inside the instrument is also set in motion; and 3) those in which two small reeds are tied together and inserted into the end of the instrument (such as the oboe) and which, when blown into, are set in motion and, subsequently, the column of air within the instrument is set in motion. The latter two types of woodwind instruments are called *single-reed* instruments and *double-reed* instruments, respectively.

Non-reed Woodwinds

Flute

The flute has no reeds, and is simply a closed pipe (closed at one end) with a hole over which the player blows to produce a sound, in much the same way one might produce a sound by blowing over the top of a soft-drink bottle. The flute also has finger holes, which are either closed or left open by the fingers, thus lengthening or shortening the column of air in the instrument, which raises or lowers the pitch. The flute also has an elaborate key mechanism, which allows the flutist (some say "flautist," although this is not common usage in the U.S.) to stop more than one hole with a single finger, or to use alternate fingerings. Usually, two to four flutes are used in the full symphony orchestra.

Piccolo

A smaller version of the flute, essentially the same as that instrument except for its size, is the *piccolo* (from the Italian *flauto piccolo*, or "little flute"). It is higher in pitch than its "big brother," the flute, demonstrating the basic rule of instruments—the smaller the instrument, the higher the pitch. There is usually only one piccolo in a symphony orchestra, and it is often played by one of the flute players of the orchestra. This is a practice referred to as *doubling*.

Single-reed Woodwinds

Clarinet

One of the most popular woodwind instruments today is the clarinet, a single-reed instrument which was not generally accepted by the orchestra until the late eighteenth century. Clarinets were occasionally included in the orchestra by the middle of the eighteenth century, although the first clarinet had been built as early as 1700.

The clarinet has a mouthpiece which is made of wood, to which a single cane reed is attached by means of a metal clamp. This mouthpiece is then inserted into the end of the instrument and the player blows into the mouthpiece, setting the reed in motion, which in turn sets the column of air inside the instrument in motion. The sound comes out the other end of the instrument, which is called the *bell* (because of its bell shape). Like the flute, the clarinet has finger holes and key mechanisms which the performer opens or closes with his fingertips, thus raising or lowering the pitch of the instrument. Usually two to four clarinets are employed in a full symphony orchestra.

Bass Clarinet

Another type of clarinet frequently included in orchestral music is the *bass clarinet*. This instrument is essentially the same as the clarinet, but much larger, and is curved at both the upper and lower parts of the instrument to accomodate this increased length. As its name implies, the bass clarinet plays lower pitches than the clarinet. Concertgoers familiar with the saxophone may mistake the bass clarinet for a type of saxophone, since it is similar to that instrument in appearance. There is only one bass clarinet in the full symphony orchestra and it is usually played by one of the clarinetists of the orchestra (doubling).

Saxophone

The *saxophone*, an instrument invented by Adolphe Sax in the nineteenth century as an extension of the clarinet concept, is an extremely popular single-reed instrument, frequently used in jazz, but an instrument which has never been accepted as a regular member of the symphony orchestra. There is an entire family of saxophones, identified as soprano, alto, tenor, baritone, and bass. The instrument is very much like a large bass clarinet in appearance (except for the soprano saxophone, which looks more like the clarinet itself), with a mouthpiece similar to the clarinet and with smaller finger holes and keys. Several French composers have included saxophones in their orchestral works, as have a number of twentieth century composers from various other countries.

Double-reed Woodwinds

The double-reed woodwinds have the oldest lineage of any wind instruments in the orchestra. Their prototypes date back to the Middle Ages. They were, in fact, the first instruments to be accepted into the early orchestras of the seventeenth century, which were originally composed entirely of string instruments.

Oboe

The principal double-reed instrument in the orchestra is the *oboe* (from the French *hautbois*, pronounced "o-bwa" and meaning "high wood"). Its mouthpiece is made of two very small and very thin

Richard Woodhams, principal oboe, The Philadelphia Orchestra.

pieces of cane reed, tied together with silk thread and inserted into the instrument. Oboists (as do most double-reed performers) usually make their own reeds. This fragile double-reed mouthpiece needs to be kept moist at all times, so the performer often keeps the reeds in his mouth when not playing. (Some oboists also keep a small vial of water nearby, in which to soak the reed.) Except for this double-reed mouthpiece, and a less-flared bell at the end of the instrument, the oboe looks very much like a clarinet. It also has a similar structure of fingerholes and keys. A versatile instrument, the oboe can produce a mournful, plaintive sound as well as a jovial, playful sound. It is considered a difficult instrument to play.

The tone of the oboe is so pure and so penetrating that it has long been the instrument which gives the pitch for the orchestra prior to the beginning of a concert, when the members of the orchestra are tuning their instruments. Two oboes are usually included in the full symphony orchestra.

English Horn

A double-reed woodwind which is essentially an alto oboe is an instrument rather curiously named the *English horn*—curious, be-

David Cramer, acting principal flute, Richard Woodhams, principal oboe, Jonathan Blumenfeld, oboe.

Jeffrey Khaner, principal flute, The Philadelphia Orchestra.

Kazuo Tokito, piccolo, The Philadelphia Orchestra.

Anthony M. Gigliotti, principal clarinet, The Philadelphia Orchestra.

Bernard Garfield, principal bassoon, The Philadelphia Orchestra.

cause it is neither English nor a horn. The term "English," with reference to this particular woodwind instrument, has an interesting story. The French, who named the instrument, called it the *Cor anglé* (pronounced "core onglay," or "angled horn"), because the earliest instruments of this type were angled in the middle. The English, subsequently, translated the name of the instrument falsely, hearing the phonetic *Cor anglais* (also pronounced "core onglay," but meaning "English horn"). Hence the unusual naming of the instrument.

The English horn has a mouthpiece similar to that of the oboe, and its sound is similar to the oboe's but is lower in pitch. The instrument was used by Haydn in his Symphony No. 22 (subtitled "The Philosopher") but was rarely used in the orchestra until the middle of the nineteenth century. The English horn is used very effectively in the slow movement of César Franck's Symphony in D Minor. A recognizable feature of the English horn is the bulbous shape of its bell. There is usually only one English horn in the full symphony orchestra, and it is often played by an oboe player as a second instrument (doubling).

Bassoon

The bass member of the double-reed woodwind family of instruments is the *bassoon*. The bassoon is actually a large oboe, but its length is so great that it is doubled upon itself, literally "folded." The Italians call the instrument *fagotto*, meaning "bundle of sticks". It is too long to be end-blown as are the oboe and English horn. The bassoon has a curved metal piece called a *bocal* inserted in its side, into which the double-reed mouthpiece is inserted. The bassoon was one of the first bass wind instruments to become a regular member of the orchestra. Usually the full symphony orchestra includes two or three bassoons.

Contrabassoon

The lowest member of the woodwind group is the contrabassoon, which is basically a bassoon greatly enlarged. It is so large, in fact, that it rests on the floor when it is played, and the bell of the instrument is turned downward. Although the bassoon has been an integral part of the orchestra for several hundred years, the contrabassoon is a nineteenth century addition. There is only one contrabassoon in the full symphony orchestra, and it is often played by a bassoonist (doubling).

Brasses

The second group of wind instruments is the brasses, instruments made either of brass or of some other metal. The use of brass instruments extends far back into music's history, and they have traditionally been associated with military activity or used in some sort of fanfare capacity. Brasses were also important in early church music, especially during the Renaissance.

The sound of brass instruments is made by "buzzing" the lips (creating a vibration much like that made by the reeds in the reed instruments), which sets in motion the column of air in the instrument. By means of various degrees of lip and air pressure (called *embouchure*, from the French *bouche*, meaning "mouth"), the brass player can play different notes. This range of notes has been greatly increased by the use of valves and keys in the evolution of brass instruments.

Trumpet

The highest in pitch of the brass instrument is the trumpet. An ancient instrument, the trumpet for most of its early history was a metal tube doubled back on itself once or twice. Different pitches were played by adjusting the pressure of the lips. In the late eighteenth century keys were added to the trumpet to allow the performer to play notes other than those which could be played through adjustment of the embouchure, or by redirecting the column of air as it flows through the instrument. In the early nineteenth century, the more complex system of valves was added to the trumpet, giving it an even greater versatility. There are usually two to four trumpets in the full symphony orchestra. The trumpet also has a collection of mutes which are inserted into the bell of the instrument in order to create a number of different tone-colors.

In the orchestra of the Classical era, the trumpet was used sparingly. Since the nineteenth century, however, it has been a frequently featured instrument in orchestral literature.

Instruments related to the trumpet are the *bugle* (with no valves), the *cornet* (smaller than the trumpet in size and somewhat less martial in sound), and the *fluegelhorn* (from the German *Fluegel*, or "wing," relating to the shape of the instrument), a brass instrument with a very mellow sound.

Horn

A brass instrument early accepted into the orchestra as being compatible with strings and woodwinds was the horn, often called the French horn, since its origins are at least partially French. The horn is so compatible with woodwind instruments that it has been included as a part of the woodwind quintet (flute, oboe, clarinet, horn, and bassoon), a popular chamber ensemble. The horn has a smaller mouthpiece than the trumpet, but a larger bell (where the sound emerges at the end of the instrument). It has much more tubing than the trumpet, but instead of being folded back on itself, like the trumpet, it is coiled into a circular form.

Glenn Dodson, principal trombone, The Philadelphia Orchestra.

There are usually four horns in the symphony orchestra and, ironically, they play in a 1-3-2-4 order from high to low, for reasons of sonority. Like the trumpet, the horn can be muted.

An earlier version of the horn, without valves, was the *posthorn*, which was used (as its name implies) as an "announcing" instrument upon the arrival of post (mail) coaches in European towns and cities. (The horn is still the symbol of the post office in Europe today.) The posthorn was and still is used as a hunting horn in fox hunts. Mozart wrote a solo for the posthorn in one of his orchestral serenades.

In the symphony orchestra the horn is played with the player's hand inserted into the bell, both to support the instrument and to subdue the sound somewhat, which explains its compatibility with the strings and woodwinds. It is also occasionally played without the player's hand inserted into the bell, when more clarion sounds are called for.

Trombone

The sound in brass instruments is raised or lowered by shortening or lengthening the column of air within the instrument. This is done in the trumpet and horn by means of a complex system of valves and interconnected tubing. The *trombone*, however, accomplishes it in the simplest way possible. The instrument is constructed with a large, curved tube, called a *slide*, which is inserted into the upper half of the instrument. The performer then pushes the slide forward or pulls it backward, as he changes his embouchure (mouth position and lip pressure) to change pitches. The bell is a component of the upper part of the instrument.

An early name for the trombone was *sackbut* (from the French *sacque-boute*). The name *trombone* is closely related to the Italian word for trumpet, which is *tromba*.

The first composer of modern orchestral music to use the trombone prominently outside the opera house was Beethoven, who included three of the instruments in the finale of his *Symphony No. 5,* in 1808.

There are usually three trombones in the full symphony orchestra, of which the third is often a bass trombone, a larger version of the trombone with a slightly lower range.

Tuba

The lowest in pitch of the brass instruments is the *tuba*, an instrument developed in the 1820s and introduced in 1835, and thus not

Frank Kaderabek, principal trumpet, The Philadelphia Orchestra.

Horn Section, The Philadelphia Orchestra, Nolan Miller, principal horn.

included in any orchestral works prior to that date (such as the symphonies of Mozart, Haydn, Schubert, and Beethoven. "Tuba" is derived from the name the ancient Romans used for a long, straight trumpet. The modern tuba, however, looks very much like a large horn squeezed into an oval shape with the bell pointed upwards. The tuba has valves like the horn and trumpet and a similar, although much larger, mouthpiece. There is usually one tuba in a full symphony orchestra. Like the other brass instruments, the tuba also has a mute—which looks very much like a small beer keg!

A larger tuba, the double-bass tuba, is occasionally used in the orchestra, and a smaller, tenor tuba, called the *euphonium*, is found more often in bands than in orchestras. The tuba most often plays the bass lines of the music being performed, but is capable of playing a warm, rich melodic line as well.

The *Wagner Tuba* is more like a modified orchestral horn than the usual tuba and is made in two sizes, tenor and bass. It was designed to Wagner's specifications for *The Ring.* The instruments were also used by Bruckner and Richard Strauss.

Paul Krzywicki, principal tuba, The Philadelphia Orchestra.

A Brass Postscript

Notice that brass performers will occasionally press a small valve at the lower part of the instrument, point the instrument toward the floor, and blow into the instrument without making any sound. This is continually necessary, because of the way in which the sound is initially produced, by buzzing the lips. This invariably causes some saliva to get into the instrument, and the performer must blow it out of his instrument to continue playing.

PERCUSSION INSTRUMENTS

The final group of instruments, often referred to as the battery of the orchestra, is the percussion instruments, so named because they are all struck percussively in some manner.

The percussion instruments fall into a variety of different categories, but for the purposes of this book, they will be considered as: drum-type instruments, vibrating instruments, and keyboard instruments.

Drum-type Instruments

Kettledrums (Timpani)

The principal instruments of this section are the kettledrums (so-named because of their kettle-like shape), which are always found in the orchestra in groups of two or more, and are frequently called *timpani*. Timpani are actually tuned, unlike other drums, by tightening or loosening the drum heads with screws which are positioned around the top of the instrument. The timpanist must have an excellent ear, since he often must quietly tune the timpani to new pitches even as the orchestra continues to play. The timpani are struck with pairs of sticks, which have either soft or hard heads, depending on the desired sound. Two methods of playing the timpani are with single strokes, or by rolling the sticks rapidly on the drumheads, creating a sound not unlike rolling thunder. Timpani have long been regular members of the orchestra and are used in combination with all instruments. They are especially effective when used with brass instruments. When they were first introduced to the orchestra in the seventeenth century, they were smaller, and most often used in combination with trumpets.

Bass and Snare Drums

Two other types of drums used in the orchestra are instruments usually thought of as belonging to the marching band, the *bass drum* and the *snare drum*. The bass drum is simply a large drum played with either one or two sticks, which have either soft or hard heads. The drum is usually struck with single strokes, but can be played with two sticks to create a drum roll similar to that of the timpani, but without pitch. The other band-derived drum is the *snare drum*, often called the *side drum*. This is a small drum, mounted on a stand when played in the orchestra. The snare drum can be played as a straight drum, with either rhythmic patterns, single strokes, or drum roll, as can the timpani and bass drum. The *snares* from which the instrument takes its name are a set of twisted strands of wire stretched across the lower head of the drum. If these snares are tightened (with a simple lever device on the instrument), a sharp, brittle sound results. If the snares are not tightened, however, the drum has a less sharp sound, more like that of a natural drum. The snare drum is used for special effects in orchestral music, and is extremely effective in music that is highly rhythmical or descriptive in nature.

Tambourine

The fourth orchestral drum-type instrument often used in the orchestra is the *tambourine*, an instrument often associated by the general public with groups like the Salvation Army. This is a small, hand-held drum, with only one drum head, and with small metal *jingles* (circular discs) inserted loosely into the instrument all around its rim. The tambourine is not struck with a beater or drumstick, but is shaken in order to set the jingles rattling, or struck with the heel of the hand in order to create both a drum sound and the sound of the jingles as well.

Vibrating Instruments

Of the percussion instruments not of the drum type, the following are instruments of the type in which the entire instrument vibrates when struck.

Cymbal(s)

The cymbal is a curved metal plate with a raised bell in its center. The cymbal is played in one of two ways: one cymbal is suspended on a stand and struck; or two cymbals, one held in each hand, are struck together. Cymbals come in a variety of sizes and thicknesses, factors that affect their sound considerably. Additionally, the suspended cymbal may be struck with any of a variety of sticks, from the hard wooden stick usually used with the snare drum to the softest yarn-covered mallet used with the vibraphone. Cymbals used as a pair (referred to either as "hand cymbals" or "crash cymbals") are generally of medium thickness and are roughly eighteen inches in diameter. Cymbals, either suspended or hand-held, are effectively used in quiet passages of music as well as at climactic moments.

Glockenspiel

The glockenspiel (also known as orchestra bells) is a set of metal bars usually made of tempered steel and mounted on a frame, which is usually attached to a portable case. Its crystalline brilliance is effective when used to double—briefly—a high melodic line or chord passage. As with other mallet instruments, it may be played with from one to four mallets, depending on whether chords or a melody is demanded.

Celesta

The celesta is a keyboard instrument which, in its elements, is very similar to the glockenspiel: it also is made up of a series of steel bars, but unlike the glockenspiel, the bars of the celesta are suspended over resonating boxes which are struck by hammers and sustained in the manner of a piano. Its sound is light and silvery, as shown by its solo use in the Dance of the Sugar-Plum Fairy in Tchaikovsky's *Nutcracker* ballet.

Chimes (Bells)

The *chimes*, or *tubular bells*. are metal tubes which are suspended from a frame and struck with a mallet. They create the sound of bells when struck, and were first used orchestrally in 1830, in Berlioz's *Symphonie fantastique*, to represent church bells.

Tam-tam (Gong)

Another instrument of this type is the *tam-tam*, or *gong*, which is constructed of a filament of metal spun out in concentric circles, a structure that allows the gong to vibrate when struck. It is usually struck with a soft beater, in single strokes, and allowed to resonate until the sound dies away.

Don S. Liuzzi, principal timpani, The Philadelphia Orchestra.

Triangle

The *triangle* is a small but effective percussion instrument. It is a resonant metal bar bent to form a triangular shape with one end open, so that the sound can escape, and is played by being suspended and struck with a metal rod. Its resonating quality is considerable, and it can be clearly heard through a large orchestral mass.

Castanets

An orchestral percussion instrument borrowed from Spanish folk music is the *castanets*, which are made of two shell-shaped pieces of resonant wood. The Spanish dancer holds the castanets with one part in the palm of his hand, manipulating the other part of the instrument with the fingers so that one strikes the other in rhythmic fashion. In orchestral performance, the castanets are often attached to a flat wooden stick, so that the percussionist can simply shake the stick to create the desired sound.

Wood Block and Cow Bell

Two very simple orchestral percussion instruments are the *wood block* and the *cow bell*. The wood block (which comes from the Orient, and is often called a Chinese block) is a hollow block of wood, open at the ends, and is usually struck with a drumstick.

The cow bell is just what its name indicates, the bell usually placed about the necks of cows to indicate where they are at any given moment. The cow bell, like the wood block, is usually mounted when used in the orchestra, and struck with a drumstick.

Ratchet

The *ratchet* is a cogwheel revolved against several tongues of wood or metal by twirling the instrument with the hand. (The instrument is similar to the noisemaker ratchet often used at parties.) Occasionally, the instrument is mounted, and the percussionist simply turns the handle. It is used to produce a special sound effect in such works as Richard Strauss' *Till Eulenspiegel*.

Keyboard Instruments

The third type of percussion instrument is the keyboard type, and includes instruments such as the *xylophone*, *marimba* and *vibraphone*.

Xylophone

The *xylophone* is made of a series of bars of resonant wood, graduated in length (the shorter the length, the higher the pitch), tuned to a scale, and placed on a frame with the bars positioned very much like the keys on a piano. The xylophone is struck with a variety of mallets, some soft and some hard. The performer is frequently required to manipulate several mallets at once, playing both melody and harmony. The bars can be struck singly, or in a rapidly-repeated fashion, creating a sustained sound.

The *marimba* is another form of the xylophone, similar in structure to that instrument, with hollow tubes of varying lengths placed under each wooden bar, perpendicular to the bar. This allows for greater resonance than is possible with the xylophone.

Vibraphone

A third keyboard-type percussion instrument is the *vibraphone*, which is similar to the marimba, except that inside each tube under each bar is a small metal disc. Through the use of an electric motor, the disc is made to spin, giving the instrument a vibrating sound not possible with either the xylophone or the marimba. It is possible to play the vibraphone with this motor turned off, and composers frequently request this sound.

Piano

An instrument that might be considered to be a percussion instrument, although its sound is produced through the vibration of strings, is the *piano*. The piano is not a regular member of the orchestra, but has been used more and more frequently in twentieth century compositions.

The piano has 88 keys which are struck by the fingers, setting in motion small hammers covered with hard felt, which strike the strings inside the instrument. Each key is also attached to a damper, which is released when the note is struck, and falls back to dampen the sound of the string when the finger is released. All these dampers can be released with the use of the right pedal on the piano (referred to as the sustaining pedal), so that the music can be sustained from note to note. The left pedal on the piano is referred to as the *una corda* pedal, since it shifts the keys so that the hammers strike only one string ("una corda") rather than all three. The middle pedal on the piano allows the pianist to selectively cause certain notes to be sustained when struck and the others to be dampened. The dampers are small pieces of hard felt, which are wedge-shaped and fall back on the strings, effectively stopping (or "damping") the sound.

The modern piano is capable of great resonance, and some contemporary composers use the piano as an orchestral rather than as a solo instrument, (its more traditional function with the symphony orchestra). In an orchestral capacity, the piano can add a certain percussive or brilliant edge to the texture.

These, then, are the instruments of the orchestra: the strings, winds, and percussion instruments. Each is unique. Combined, they create the magnificent sound of the modern symphony orchestra.

Alan Abel, associate principal percussion, The Philadelphia Orchestra.

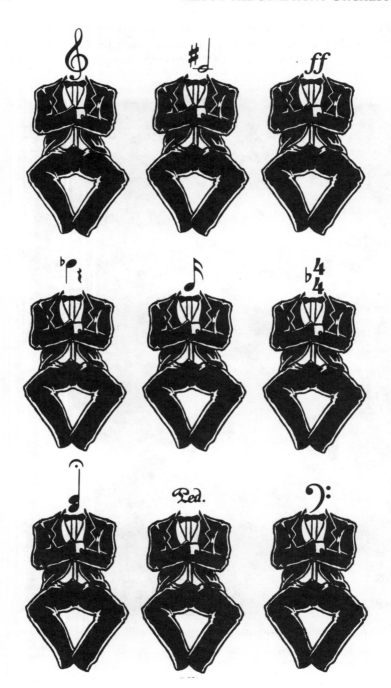

Chapter 4

THE LANGUAGE OF ORCHESTRAL MUSIC

The four basic elements of music are rhythm, melody, harmony, and texture. Of these, the most basic is rhythm.

RHYTHM

As rhythm is a basic element of life—as experienced in our breathing, our heartbeats, the ticking of a clock, days and nights, the seasons, and life cycles—so is the element of rhythm basic to music as well.

The initial response one usually has to the rhythm of a piece of music is to its *pulse*, or *beat*. It is this that sets toes tapping or bodies swaying. An element of the pulse of music is the speed at which the music is being played. The musical term for this is *tempo*. It is helpful that the listener should have a knowledge of tempo markings in music, since a great many orchestral works, or movements of orchestral works, are identified only by their tempo markings. By understanding the meaning of these tempo markings, the listener knows before the music begins how fast or slow it will be.

A few of the most common tempo markings used in orchestral music are:

PRESTO	Extremely fast
VIVACE	Quite fast, lively
ALLEGRO	Fast
MODERATO	Moderate tempo
ANDANTE	"Walking" tempo
LENTO	Rather slow
ADAGIO	Slow

Other qualifying terms, such as *molto* (very) or *non troppo* (not too much), are often coupled with the above tempo markings. To learn more of these terms, make note of any new terms appearing on concert programs and look them up in the glossary of terms in Chapter Six. In this way your music vocabulary will grow every time you attend a concert.

Another aspect of rhythm with which the listener should be acquainted is *meter*. The beats (pulse) of the music, regardless of tempo, are usually grouped into twos or threes, or their multiples. (Groups of fours and sixes are quite common). These are called *duple* (two) or *triple* (three) meter. The first beat of each *measure* (the name given to a group of beats) is usually accented, ONE-two-three, or ONE-two-three-four. Too much accent, of course, would be unmusical, and accents would be emphasized only in such music as a rousing march or lively waltz. The meter can also be followed by watching the conductor, since his downbeat is always the first beat of a measure. (Refer to the discussion of the conductor's beats in Chapter One.)

One final thing about rhythm: a shifting of accents from the normal first beat of the measure is often used by composers to give the rhythm more vitality and variety. This shifting of the normal accent is called *syncopation*.

MELODY

The next reaction one usually has to music is to its *melody*. In orchestral music this is particularly important. Recognizing the principal melodic line of a composition is an easy way to follow the overall structure of the music, since most orchestral music is written through the use of a melody or melodies and the development of, and reappearance of, those melodies.

The melodic material of most orchestral music is of two types. The first of these is called a *motive*, which is an extremely short fragment used by the composer. The most famous motive in orchestral music is the opening notes of Beethoven's *Fifth Symphony,* a motive composed of only four notes, three of which are the same pitch. A more common type of melodic line, however, is the *theme*, which is longer than a motive. Often, the composer presents one or two themes (contrasting in style, so that the listener can easily differentiate between them), develops these themes in a variety of ways, and then repeats them, bringing the music to a close. This represents a basic musical form used in orchestral music, *sonata form*, which will be discussed in detail in Chapter Five.

Thus, although the rhythm of a piece of music is its most basic element, it is the melodic material of the music, its motives and themes, that the listener remembers, and that enable him to recognize the work when he hears it again.

HARMONY

The third basic element of orchestral music is its *harmony*. If rhythm is the heart of music and melody its soul, then harmony is the flesh and bones that make the music complete. It is the full, rich harmonic sound of the symphony orchestra that brings audiences again and again to the concert hall to hear more of the same.

The basic element of harmony is the *chord*, three or more notes sounding together. Chords can be built on any note, and can be inverted, combined, and used in an infinite number of ways to create that great body of sound known as harmony. It is possible for harmony to be stringent to the ear (*dissonant*) or pleasant to the ear (*consonant*), but most orchestral music presents a blend of consonance and dissonance, creating the tension and relaxation that makes orchestral music so exciting.

Melody and harmony are most often combined according to certain musical laws to create music that is *tonal*. Tonality implies that there is a specific musical pitch around which the composition is built, a kind of "home base" as it were. It is for this reason that most orchestral works are listed as being in the *key* (i.e., *tonality*) of C, or D, or B-flat, for example.

Also, tonality can be structured in two ways depending on the specific notes of the scale being used, *major* or *minor*. This is an aspect of tonality known as *mode*. The principal difference in sound between major and minor is that in minor, the third and sixth pitches of the scale are lowered. It is often very wrongly stated that minor implies sadness and major implies happiness. Major and minor are merely two different aspects of tonality, or key. Either can be made "happy" or "sad" by the way they are used by the composer, but the mood of music is rarely determined solely by the use of the major or minor mode.

TEXTURE

The last basic element of music is its texture. The three textures commonly used in orchestral music are *monophonic, homophonic,* and *polyphonic*.

Monophonic music is a single melodic line, with no harmony. It can be played by a single instrument, or by the entire orchestra, but is monophonic only if no harmony is present. Monophonic texture is used in orchestral music for contrast, often to create an incisive feeling, or perhaps a transparent mood.

Homophonic texture is made up of a dominant melodic line and a harmonic structure that is secondary to the melody and serves as its *accompaniment*.

The most complex kind of musical texture is *polyphonic,* which is made up of two or more independent melodic lines played simultaneously. Harmony is created, but each melodic line retains its melodic independence. Polyphonic texture is very common in music of the Renaissance and Baroque periods of music (1450-1750), as in the music of Palestrina or Bach, but is often found in music of later periods as well.

Most orchestral music uses a combination of all three of these textures (usually with a stronger emphasis on homophonic), to create a textural balance and to achieve variety and color.

Other Musical Elements

An element of music basic to its performance is that of loudness and softness, referred to in music as *dynamics.* Italian terms are often used in referring to dynamics in music. The two basic terms are *forte* (loud) and *piano* (soft). The term for very soft is *pianissimo* and the term for very loud is *fortissimo. Crescendo* indicates that the music is getting gradually louder and *diminuendo* (occasionally *decrescendo*) indicates that the music is becoming gradually softer. These terms rarely occur in concert programs, however, and are presented here for general information.

Another element of music to consider is one that relates directly to the previous chapter on musical instruments. This is *tone color*, for which the French term *timbre* (pronounced TAM-ber) is usually used. Tone color, or timbre, enables the listener to distinguish the sound of a violin from that of a horn, even when they are playing the same note. It involves a complex system of fundamentals and overtones too involved to be explained in any detail here. It is a good practice for the concertgoer, nonetheless, to try to develop an awareness of the timbre of various instruments or groups of instruments, eventually knowing instinctively which way to look when a specific sound emanates from the orchestra. An excellent orchestral work that teaches the various timbres of the orchestra is the English composer Benjamin Britten's *The Young Person's Guide to the Orchestra*, subtitled *Variations and Fugue on a Theme of Purcell*.

Summary

This, then, is a bit of the language of music. Terms like rhythm, meter, tempo, melody, motive, theme, harmony, chord, tonality, major, minor, dynamics, and timbre should give the listener a broader comprehension of music.

Form—"Music's Architecture," Philharmonic Center for the Arts, Naples, Florida, Myra Janco Daniels, President and C.E.O.

PHOTO: © ARTHUR D'ARAZIEN

Chapter 5

MAJOR FORMS OF COMPOSITION FOR THE SYMPHONY ORCHESTRA

The term *form* in music is used to denote structure or architecture—whether it be the overall form of the composition, or the internal structure of one *movement* of a composition. An understanding of the musical form can be a great help to the listener in following the music as it is performed, and will assist the listener in knowing what to expect. A few of the most frequently used forms will be discussed in this chapter.

The two basic types of overall orchestral forms are single-movement compositions and multi-movement compositions. The term *movement* may date from a time when instrumental music was primarily used to accompany dancing in which each separate section of the music accompanied a specific dance movement, thus the term *movement* came to represent a part of a larger section of instrumental music. Each of these individual parts, or movements, has a specific internal form — the structure in which it is written.

When a multi-movement work, such as a symphony or concerto, is performed, it is not complete until all the movements have been played, usually four movements in a symphony and three movements in a concerto. Applause should be withheld until *all* movements have been played.

SINGLE-MOVEMENT COMPOSITIONS

Overture

The most frequently-performed single-movement orchestral work is the *overture*, often referred to as a curtain-raiser, since it is usually programmed at the beginning of a concert. Overtures can be of many types. Overtures from operas are frequently played, as are overtures written for nineteenth-century plays, a common practice at that time. Beethoven wrote several overtures of this type, such as the *Egmont* overture. These works are occasionally called theatrical or dramatic overtures because they originated as music written for dramas. Overtures can also be written specifically for concert performances; these are usually referred to as *concert overtures*.

Symphonic Poem

Another type of single-movement orchestral work is the *tone poem*, or *symphonic poem*, a form established by the great nineteenth-century virtuoso pianist and composer Franz Liszt, but brought to its apex by the German composer-conductor Richard Strauss. The tone poem has no text, as the term might imply, but can be based on a poem, as was Liszt's *Les Préludes*. A tone poem can have a story line, like Strauss' *Till Eulenspiegel's Merry Pranks*, be descriptive of a personality, like Strauss' *Don Juan* and *Don Quixote*, the latter of which also has a story line, or be descriptive of a place, like Strauss' *Aus Italien*.

These are programmatic works, which implies that an extramusical meaning is being suggested by the composer. Since, however, such extramusical ideas are rarely so obvious in the music that all listeners perceive them, the composer often writes a description, that can be included in the program book given to the audience.

MULTI-MOVEMENT COMPOSITIONS

The Suite

Of the orchestral multi-movement works, the *suite* is one of the oldest. The suite (taken from the French *suivez* "to follow") consists of a series of short pieces which are in some way related, either musically or, if the suite is programmatic, extramusically.

The earliest suites were usually a series of dances, which is probably the origin (as mentioned earlier in this chapter) of the use of the term *movement* for the various parts of a multi-movement work, since each particular dance had its own special movement. The earliest dance suites were often for keyboard instruments, particularly the harpsichord. A common combination of dances at that time include an *Allemande* (a German dance), *Courante* (a French dance), *Sarabande* (a Spanish dance), and *Gigue* (a dance from the British Isles), thus making the early dance suite quite international in character.

Suites were not, however, limited to collections of dances, but soon became a popular multi-movement form. Bach's great contemporary Handel wrote two popular works from which suites were extracted, one for a royal regatta which he called the *Water Music*, and one for a royal celebration featuring a fireworks display which he called the *Royal Fireworks Music*.

Suites are sometimes made up from collections from theatrical incidental music, from instrumental versions of operas, and from many other varied sources. The wide realm of possibilities for the writing of a suite has made it a popular form for composers as well as for audiences.

Frequently, music taken from other forms, such as ballet, opera or incidental music for a dramatic presentation, is made into an orchestral suite. The most common suite of this type is the ballet suite, made up of excerpts from a ballet score. The various parts of the ballet selected for the suite are most often arranged in the order in which they occur in the original ballet. A notable example is the frequently-performed *Nutcracker* suite from Tchaikovsky's ballet *The Nutcracker*. In the newly-formed suite, the various sections bear the titles of the various scenes of the ballet from which they are taken.

Another type of suite derived from a different musical form is the opera suite. In this type of suite, various arias or other musical numbers, such as duets, ensembles or choruses, are extracted from a particular opera; the text is often put aside, and the new suite emerges as an orchestral work. Usually the overture of the opera is used as the opening movement of the opera suite. Unlike the ballet suite, however, in which the various parts of the suite are identified by the scenes of the ballet from which they are taken, the movements of an opera suite are not usually given titles relating to the opera. A notable example of an opera suite is that derived from Bizet's popular opera *Carmen*.

A third type of suite taken from a pre-existing form is the suite of incidental music. During the nineteenth century, composers were often commissioned to write music for plays, in the form of overtures, entr'acte music or, occasionally, background music to be played during the performance of the play itself. Many theatrical suites continue to be performed as orchestral works long after the play for which they were written has been performed and perhaps even forgotten. Popular examples are the two *Peer Gynt* suites, taken from the music written by the Norwegian composer Edvard Grieg for theatrical productions of Henrik Ibsen's national saga of the same name. Similarly, Bizet's *L'Arlésienne* suites are based on music written for the all-but-forgotten play entitled *The Woman of Arles*.

The Concerto

One of the most popular multi-movement forms today is the concerto, which features a solo instrument in dialogue with the symphony orchestra. The most popular types of concertos are those for piano or violin, but concertos have been written for most of the instruments of the orchestra, as well as for some instruments not a part of the standard orchestra.

The term *concerto* (also related to the term *concert*) comes from the Italian word *concertato*, which is a term used during the Baroque era to indicate a musical structure made up of at least two different elements which joined forces (i.e. made a concerted effort) to produce a musical whole. During the Baroque era there were three basic kinds of concerto. The first was the *orchestra concerto*, in which the orchestra was divided into two equal parts to perform in a kind of antiphonal, or dialogue, fashion. The second concerto type of this era, and one of the most popular, was the *concerto grosso*, which featured a small group of soloists, numbering from two to five (the *concertino* group), and the larger orchestra (the *ripieno group*), which played in dialogue fashion. When the two groups played together the term used was *tutti* (Italian for "all"). The third type of concerto was the *solo concerto*, which featured a solo instrument in dialogue with the full orchestra. The great master of the second type of concerto was Johann Sebastian Bach, especially in his *Brandenburg Concertos*, and the great master of the solo concerto during the Baroque era was the Italian composer Antonio Vivaldi, who wrote more than five hundred concertos for nearly every instrument in the orchestra, and some non-orchestral instruments, such as the mandolin.

The solo concerto has become one of the most popular concert program selections today, because of its structure and, especially, because it allows the showcasing of virtuoso soloists.

Concertos often have three movements, usually in a fast-slow-fast format. The first movement is most likely to be in a somewhat modified sonata form. In the late eighteenth century, the concerto featured a *double exposition*, in which the orchestra played an exposition of sorts, but which left the "second theme" to the soloist for his first entrance. A feature of most concertos is the *cadenza* (from the musical term *cadence*, or closing formula) which occurs very close to the end of the movement. The orchestra stops playing and the soloist plays alone. In early concertos, the soloist was expected to improvise at this point, but from Beethoven onward composers began to write out the cadenza, so that the soloist could not take liberties with the music. Cadenzas usually occur in the first movement, but are occasionally found in the finale and even in the second movement.

The Symphony

The principal multi-movement work in the orchestra repertoire is the symphony, from which most major orchestras today take their name. The term actually refers to a piece of music, not to an orchestra. To call an orchestra a *symphony* is like calling it a *concerto*, perhaps, which is misleading, but calling it a *symphony orchestra* (which is more common today) is also somewhat inaccurate, since it implies the orchestra plays only symphonies, which is untrue.

The symphony as we know it is derived from the seventeenth century Italian opera overture. Monteverdi in 1607 decided to open his opera *Orfeo* with a setting in three sections of a simple chord, which may be in imitation of the traditional three knocks that announced the beginning of a play in those days. The opera overture, or *sinfonia*, eventually developed into a three-part work in a fast-slow-fast format. These three sections were expanded into three separate movements, still in the fast-slow-fast format, and soon thereafter the *sinfonia* was separated from its connection with the opera to become an independent orchestral work.

The earliest symphonies (Sammartini, early Haydn) maintained this three-movement structure, but during the eighteenth century a popular dance form, the *minuet*, was inserted between the slow second movement and the fast finale. In the nineteenth century, beginning with Beethoven, this minuet was developed beyond the confines of the dance form, and began to be called *scherzo* (which is, curiously, the Italian word for "joke").

The first movement of the symphony is in sonata form, often with an introduction at the beginning and a coda at the end. The second movement is usually slow (*andante*, a slow walking tempo, is the most commonly-used tempo). The third movement, the minuet (or scherzo), is frequently in triple meter, as was the original dance; this movement has a middle section called the *trio*, so called because in the earliest orchestral minuets, this middle section was played by only three instruments, to create textural contrast. Although in later works the use of only three instruments was dropped, this middle section continues to be called *trio*. The structure of the minuet (or scherzo) movement, then, is three-part form, minuet-trio-minuet (ABA).

The last movement of the symphony, usually called the *finale* (from the Italian *fine,* "close" or "end"), is most often in a fast tempo, as is the first movement. Eighteenth century composers frequently set this movement as a rondo, but nineteenth century composers used different forms, including sonata form or even passacaglia (as in the Brahms Symphony No. 4).

In concert programs, symphonic movements are indicated by tempo markings (such as *allegro, adagio,* etc.), unless the symphony is programmatic, in which case specific titles will be given each movement. Using the glossary of terms in Chapter 6 of this book, the concertgoer can know at what tempo and in which mood each movement will be performed by referring to the tempo markings for each movement.

Orchestral music is always more enjoyable to listen to if one is aware of the musical form and structure. Being familiar with structure allows the listener to follow the music more closely and to better appreciate and understand its various parts. Such awareness can greatly enhance the overall listening experience.

INDIVIDUAL MOVEMENT FORMS

Whether the composition is a single-movement or multi-movement work, each movement has an individual form. The following are the most common.

Theme and Variations

A popular type of single-movement orchestral music is the theme-and-variation form. A prominent musical theme, or melody (often borrowed from another composer, usually to honor him), is presented in a variety of different ways, using different instrumentation, different rhythms and altered melodic material. If the original theme, or melody, is altered so much that the original tune is no longer recognizable, the set of variations is said to be *implicit*. If, however, the original tune is readily recognizable in all of the variations, the set of variations is referred to as *explicit*.

The Strauss tone poem *Don Quixote*, previously mentioned in the discussion of overtures, is also a set of variations on, as Strauss indicates, "a knightly theme." As noted earlier, composers often honor their predecessors in their choice of a theme for variation form, as in Brahms' *Variations on a Theme of Haydn* (actually an even older chorale tune that Haydn used) or Rachmaninov's popular *Rhapsody on a Theme of Paganini* (the great nineteenth century violinist/composer). Theme-and-variations form is popular with composers because it allows them relatively free reign of their creative imaginations, with few formal restrictions.

Rondo Form

Another single-movement type, but one that is usually included as part of a multi-movement form (such as a symphony or concerto), is the *rondo*. Rondo is a structure in which an initially-stated theme recurs throughout the work, with interspersed contrasting musical statements. These statements in the orchestral rondo form are usually called *episodes*.

Musical form is often graphed with the use of letters of the alphabet (having no reference to keys, however), such as A, B, C, D, etc., the letter changing each time a new musical section appears. In rondo form, for example, "A" would represent the rondo theme itself and other letters would represent the interspersed episodes. A typical rondo letter graph would thus be ABACADA.

Rondo form, or the hybrid sonata-rondo form, was typically used for the final movement of a symphony or concerto during the Classical era (the period of Haydn and Mozart).

Sonata Form

The most basic and widely-used musical form for a single movement is *sonata* form. The term *sonata* comes from the Italian word *sonare* (to sound), and related, in the sixteenth and seventeenth centuries, to all instrumental music (music without words), as opposed to vocal music (music with words), usually referred to at that time as *cantata* (from *cantare*, meaning "to sing").

Sonata is a term also used with reference to works for solo instruments, particularly keyboard instruments. The first movements of these solo sonatas were cast in a particular form that has given sonata form its name. (It is, in fact, often called *first-movement form* for this reason).

Sonata form has three basic parts, and can be graphed ABA. The first section ("A") is referred to as the *exposition*. In the exposition the theme or themes of the movement are presented, or exposed, as the term implies. In the "B" section, called the *development*, these themes are manipulated in some manner. Following the development section, the theme or themes are presented again, in a manner recognizably similar to their presentation in the exposition. This final section is called the *recapitulation.*

These three sections, exposition-development-recapitulation, constitute the basic structure of sonata form. Although employed particularly in first movements of multi-movement works, sonata form is also frequently used for any of the movements in many orchestral works.

Additions to sonata form include an *introduction* at the beginning of the movement, prior to the beginning of the exposition. If the exposition is fast, as it usually is, the introduction, especially in the symphonies of Haydn, is usually slow. Another addition to sonata form is the *coda* (from the Italian word for "tail"), at the close of the movement, following the recapitulation.

Forms Built Over The Bass Line

During the Baroque era (1600-1750) a number of forms were used in which the music was essentially a set of variations built over a repeated bass line. Two such forms frequently used were the *passacaglia* and the *chaconne.* In both cases a bass line, with or without its harmonic structure, is continuously repeated, and a variety of musical structures is written over this bass line, as in theme and variations form.

Bach was a great master of these forms. An important example of such a form in the nineteenth century is the final movement of the *Symphony No. 4* of Johannes Brahms.

Free Forms

In addition to these structured forms, there are a number of musical works which have little or no predetermined structure, and are usually referred to as *free forms.* Examples of such free forms are *rhapsody, fantasia, prelude*, etc.

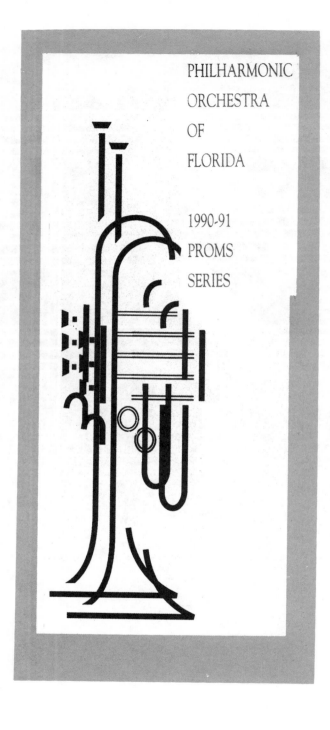

PHILHARMONIC
ORCHESTRA
OF
FLORIDA

1990-91
PROMS
SERIES

Chapter 6

WHAT YOU LEARN FROM A CONCERT PROGRAM

The combinations of symphonic works that might be selected for a concert are endless. Most programs offer a variety of styles, forms, and composers. The Music Director has the overall responsibility for program selection. On special occasions, an entire concert may be devoted to the music of one composer or period of music.

The Concert Program

The programs of most orchestral concerts include three or four works. The following are examples of programs offering a variety of literature:

1. A program with a guest soloist:

Overture to "The Magic Flute"—Mozart
Piano Concerto No. 3 in C Minor—Beethoven

INTERMISSION

Symphonie fantastique—Berlioz

2. An all-orchestral program:

Water Music—Handel
Symphony No. 40 in G Minor—Mozart

INTERMISSION

Ein Heldenleben—Strauss

The program books provided at these concerts often include program notes about each work to be performed. Historical and background information on the composer and the specific work may be highlighted and the nature and form of the music summarized.

Movement designations, whether they simply indicate the tempo or are more descriptive of some aspect of the music, may appear in any of several languages. Italian, French, and German are perhaps the most common; an example follows in each of these respective languages:

> Symphony No. 5 in C Minor—Beethoven
>   Allegro con brio (lively with spirit)
>   Andante con moto (a walking pace with motion)
>   Allegro (lively)
>   Finale: Allegro (final movement: lively)

> La Mer (The Sea)—Debussy
>   I. De l'aube à midi sur la mer
>   (From dawn to noon at sea)
>   II. Jeux de vagues
>   (Play of waves)
>   III. Dialogue du vent et de la mer
>   (Dialogue of the wind and the sea)

> Symphony No.1 in D Major—Mahler

>   I.   Langsam. Schleppend. Wie ein Naturlaut
>   (slowly, drawn out like a sound of nature)
>   II. Kräftig bewegt, doch nicht zu schnell
>   (strongly agitated, but not too fast)
>   III. Feierlich und gemessen, ohne zu schleppen
>   (solemn and measured, without dragging)
>   IV. Stürmisch bewegt
>   (stormily agitated)

In addition to the Italian terms, Beethoven also used descriptive titles in his *Symphony No. 6 in F Major* (*Pastoral*) as follows:

I.   Cheerful impressions awakened by arrival in the country
II. Scene by the brook
III. Merry gathering of country folk
IV. Thunderstorm: tempest
V.   Shepherds' Song; glad and grateful feelings after the storm.

A glossary of Italian, French, and German terms commonly used in symphonic compositions follows. It should prove helpful in defining the tempo and style of each movement.

GLOSSARY OF TERMS

A

Adagio–slow, leisurely.
Affettuoso–tenderly.
Al fine–to the end.
Alla breve–duple meter.
Allegretto–lively, but not as lively as allegro.
Allegro–lively, at a quick pace.
Allegro assai–very fast.
Allegro non troppo–not too lively or quickly.
Andante–going, at a moderate tempo, a walking pace.
Andantino–slightly faster than andante.
Animato–spirited.
Appassionato–passionate.
Arioso–melodic, expressive vocal style.
Assai–very.
Assez–fairly.

B

Barbaro–savage.
Beaucoup–very much.
Beleben–to animate.
Belebt–brisk, animated.
Bewegt–with motion.
Bittend–pleading.
Bleiben–to remain.
Breit–broad.
Brio–spirit.
Brillante–sparkling.
Burlesco–jesting, light.

C

Cantabile–in a singing manner.

Campanella–a little bell.
Capo–the head or beginning; the top.
Coda–a concluding section of a movement or work.
Comodo–conveniently, easily, with composure.
Con–with.
Con brio–with spirit.
Con fuoco–with fire.
Con moto–with motion.
Con spirito–with spirit.
Crescendo–increasing in volume of sound; indicated by the sign $<$

D

Da capo–repeat from the beginning, usually in a minuet. At end of
   middle section (B), repeat (A) section.
Da capo al fine–repeat from the beginning to the designated ending
   (*fine*).
Dal segno–from the sign (𝄋   ); a mark directing a repetition from
   the indicated point.
Deciso–in a bold and decided manner.
Diminuendo–diminishing gradually the intensity or power of the
   tone, indicated by the sign $>$
Doloroso–dolorously, sorrowfully, sadly.
Doppio movimento–double movement of time (twice as fast).

E

Eine–a, an, one.
Einfach–simple, plain.
Energico–energetic, vigorous, forceful.
Eroica–heroic.
Espressivo–with expression.
Etude–a study, exercise.
Etwas–somewhat, little.

F

Feierlich–solemn, stately.
Feroce–fierce; with an expression of ferocity.
Finale–last movement of a symphony or concerto.
Fine–the end.
Flessibile–flexible, pliant.
Forza–force, strength, power.

Fröhlich—joyous, gay.
Funebre—funeral, mournful.
Fuoco—fire, spirit.
Für—for.
Furioso—furious, vehement, angry.

G

Gai—gay, merry.
Galante—gallantly, boldly.
Ganz—whole, entire.
Gemächlich—quietly; in a calm manner.
Giocoso—humorously, sportively.
Giusto—steady, exact.
Grandioso—grand, noble.
Grave—serious, slow and solemn.
Grazioso—gracefully.
Grosso—full, great, grand.

H

Hurtig—quick, swiftly (similar to allegro).

I

Immer—always, ever.
Impetuoso—impetuous, vehement.
Intrepido—intrepid, bold.

J

Jeu—play.

K

Kräftig—powerful; vigorous, full of energy.

L

Lagrimoso—weeping; tearful; in a sad and mournful style.
Lamentoso—mournful.
Ländlich—rural.
Languido—languishing, feeble.

Langsam—slow.
Largamente—broadly, fully.
Larghetto—not quite as slow as largo.
Largo—broad, slow.
Lebhaft—lively.
Légèrement—lightly, nimbly, gaily.
Lieblich—lovely, charming.
Lobgesang—a hymn or song of praise.
Lontano—distant, remote.
Lugubre—lugubrious, sad, mournful.
Lustig—merrily, cheerfully, gaily.

M

Maestoso—majestically.
Main—hand.
Main droite—right hand.
Main gauche—left hand.
Malinconia—in a melancholy style.
Marziale—martial, military.
Mässig—moderately.
Militaire—military: in a martial style.
Meno—less.
Meno mosso—less movement.
Moderato—in moderate time.
Molto—very.
Molto allegro—very fast.
Moto—motion.
Mosso—moved, agitated.
Movimento—motion, movement, impulse; the time of a piece.
Misterioso—mysteriously.
Mutig—courageous, spirited.

N

Non—not, no.
Non troppo—not too much, moderately.

O

Ostinato—a melodic or rhythmic figure repeated persistently.
Ou—or.

P

Passionato—passionate, impassioned; with fervor and pathos.
Patetico—pathetic, with feeling.
Piacere—to be played at the pleasure of the performer.
Più—more.
Più allegro—faster.
Più mosso—moved, quicker.
Pomposo—pompous, stately, grand.
Preciso—precise, exact.
Presto—very fast, quick.

Q

Quasi—somewhat, in the style of.

R

Recitative—a musical declamation.
Religioso—religiously, solemnly; in a devout manner.
Rigore—rigor; strictness of tempo.
Risoluto—resolute, bold.
Rubato—a give and take in tempo—the performer now hurrying
    ahead, now lingering, to achieve a personal quality of expression.
Ruhig—peacefully.
Rustico—rural, rustic.

S

Scherzando—playful, lively, sportive, merry.
Schnell—quick.
Schwer—heavily, ponderously.
Sciolto—free, light.
Sehr—very, much, extremely.
Sempre—always, continually.
Sentimento—feeling, sentiment; with delicate expression.
Serioso—serious, grave.
Solenne—solemn.
Sostenuto—sustained, in a fairly slow tempo.
Sotto voce—softly; in an undertone.
Spasshaft—sportively, playfully, merrily.
Spirito—spirit, life, energy.

Stark—strong, loud, vigorous.
Stesso—the same.
Strepitoso—noisy, boisterous.
Stridente—sharp, shrill, acute.
Stück—piece, air, tune.
Suave—in a gentle, soft and engaging style.
Subito—suddenly, at once.

T

Tanto—so much, as much.
Tanz—a dance.
Tardamente—slowly.
Tempestoso—tempestuous, stormy, boisterous.
Tempo—rate of speed of a piece or a section of a work. Tempo markings range from slow to fast.
Tempo giusto—strict time.
Tempo ordinario—ordinary or moderate time.
Tempo primo—first or original tempo.
Tempo rubato—robbed time; irregular time.
Teneramente—tenderly, delicately.
Tenuto—sustained.
Timoroso—timorous, with hesitation.
Toujours—always.
Tranquillo—tranquil, calm, quiet.
Traurig—heavily, sadly, mournfully.
Très—very, most.
Tristezza—sadness, heaviness, pensiveness.
Tronco—cut short.
Troppo—too much.
Turca—Turkish.
Tutta la forza—with all possible force, as loud and forceful as possible.
Tutti—all, the entire ensemble.

U

Uguale—equal, like, similar.
Umore—humor, playful.

V

Veloce—swiftly.
Velocissimo—very swiftly, with extreme rapidity.
Vibrato—a strong, vibrating, full quality of tone; resonant.
Viel—much; a great deal.
Vigoroso—vigorous, bold, energetic.
Violento—violent, vehement, boisterous.
Vivace—quick, lively, vivacious.

W

Wehmutig—sad, sorrowful.
Wirdig—dignified.
Wuchtig—weightily, ponderously.
Wut—madness, rage.

Z

Zart–Zärtlich—tenderly, softly, delicately.
Ziemlich—tolerably, moderately.
Zierlich—neat, graceful.
Zingara—gypsy style.
Zingaresa—gypsy music.
Zu—at, by, in, to, unto.
Zwei—two.

FORMS AS TITLES OF MOVEMENTS

The following terms are sometimes used as titles of movements of a larger work and indicate the genre, as well as the style and character, of the music:

Air—a melody or tune, sometimes the title of a short melodic movement.

Aria—an elaborate solo, for voice or an instrument with accompaniment, usually from a larger work.

Ballade—a musical setting of a romantic narrative poem, or an instrumental work of that character.

Barcarolle—a piece in the style of a boat song, usually in moderate $\frac{6}{8}$ meter.

Berceuse—a cradle song, lullaby.

Bolero—a Spanish dance in triple meter.

Cavatina—a melody, sung or played in the style of a simple, short song.

Chaconne—a piece in moderately slow triple meter in which a chord progression serves as the foundation for a series of variations.

Chorale—a hymn tune, or a piece in that style in which all of the parts generally move together in chordal style.

Elegy—a song of lamentation.

Etude—a piece intended to advance one's technical mastery.

Fantasia—a work in free form in an improvisatory style.

Farandole—a dance of Provence (region of southern France, once an independent country) originally accompanied by pipe and tabor.

Fugue—a contrapuntal composition featuring the entries of all voices (instruments) in imitation of each other, somewhat in the manner of a round, except more intricately developed.

Gavotte—an old dance in ⁴⁄₄ time beginning on the third beat of the measure.

Gopak—Russian folk dance in quick ²⁄₄ time.

Habanera—Cuban dance of Spanish origin.

Hymn—a song of praise or of supplication.

Intermezzo—a short lyric piece of a romantic character.

Ländler—a variant of the waltz, originating in rural Austria.

Minuet (Eng.), *Menuet* (Fr.), *Minuetto* (It.)—A dance in triple time of French rustic origin, the standard third movement of the classical-era symphony.

Nocturne—a short lyric composition: tender, personal and free form.

Passacaglia—similar to the Chaconne, except that the variations are woven above/around a one-line melody rather than a chord progression. The difference between a Passacaglia and Chaconne is not always well-defined.

Pavane—slow stately dance, dating from sixteenth century.

Polacca—Polish national dance in triple meter.

Polka—a nineteenth-century Bohemian dance in duple time.

Potpourri—a medley of favorite musical pieces.

Rhapsody—free form, generally suggestive of some kind of romantic "inspiration."

Recitative—"musical speech," instrumental or vocal; a passage having the free, non-metric character of speech (recitation).

Romance—usually a slow piece in which intimacy and tenderness are implied.

Rondo—a piece in which the recurrence of a theme alternates with contrasting themes—i.e., A B A C A D A. Often the last movement of a symphony or concerto.

Rondino—a short piece in the form of a rondo.

Scherzo—a lively movement frequently in triple time. Scherzo means "joke" in Italian.

Tema—theme or subject.

Totenmarsch—funeral march.

Trio—middle section (B) of a dance movement or scherzo—usually slightly more singing (melodic) in style compared to the more rhythmic minuet or scherzo.

Vorspiel—prelude, introductory movement.

Waltz—popular dance of nineteenth century in ¾ time used in many works.

Wiegenlied—cradle song.

Zigeunerlied—gypsy song.

Chapter 7

MAJOR ORCHESTRAL COMPOSERS— THEIR LIVES AND WORKS

JOHANN SEBASTIAN BACH (1685-1750)

Born in Eisenach, Germany, Bach was a member of a musical family stretching back for nearly two hundred years. He was principally an organist and choir director, but wrote orchestral music as well. He held music positions in Mühlhausen, in Cöthen (where he wrote some of his important orchestral music, since his work there was primarily involved with the court orchestra), in Weimar, and in Leipzig (where he spent the major part of his adult creative life).

The orchestra for which Bach composed was quite small, by today's standards, and rarely exceeded twenty-five members. It was principally a string orchestra, with oboes, bassoons, flutes (Bach usually used the instrument known today as the recorder) and, occasionally, trumpets and timpani.

Bach's orchestral works include four suites. Suite No. 3 contains the familiar melody commonly referred to as "Air for G-String" because the nineteenth century violin virtuoso Wilhelm once played the entire melody on the G string of his violin. Another important collection of Bach's orchestral music is the set of six concertos known as the *Brandenburg Concertos*, because they were submitted by Bach to the Elector of Brandenburg (in Prussia) in hopes of obtaining a musical position in that court. Other Bach orchestral works include several harpsichord concertos, including works for two, three, and four harpsichords. Several of these were arranged from violin works of the Italian composer Vivaldi, whose work Bach greatly admired. Bach also wrote concertos for violin and oboe, and a triple concerto for flute, violin, and harpsichord.

Bach was married twice. His first wife was his cousin Maria Barbara Bach, and his second wife was the singer Anna Magdalena Wülcken. No fewer than twenty (!) children were born to these marriages, although only nine children survived infancy, owing to the high mortality rate for children in the early eighteenth century. Two of Bach's children became prominent musicians in their own right; the second eldest, Carl Philipp Emmanuel, and the youngest, Johann Christian. The eldest son, Wilhelm Friedemann, Bach's "beloved son," was a gifted musician and composer, but had a profligate life style that kept him from achieving any degree of success as either a performer or a composer.

SAMUEL BARBER (1910-1981)

Barber was born in West Chester, Pennsylvania, and received his musical training at the Curtis Institute in Philadelphia, as a member of its first graduating class. He was active as a singer, pianist, and composer. Barber's compositional style is traditional, tonal, and thoroughly romantic.

Barber's first work for orchestra was an overture for the Sheridan play *The School for Scandal*. His most popular orchestral work, however, is undoubtedly his *Adagio for Strings*, an orchestral arrangement of the second movement of his string quartet. He composed two symphonies. His cello concerto won the 1947 New York Music Critics Award and his 1962 piano concerto won the Pulitzer Prize. Barber's other orchestral works include a violin concerto and his *Capricorn* Concerto (named after his home in New York State), which is for flute, oboe, trumpet, and string orchestra, and three *Essays* for orchestra.

BÉLA BARTÓK (1881-1945)

Bartók was born in Nagyszentmiklós, Hungary (which is today Sînnicolau Mare, Romania). He was active as a pianist and composer, and in addition to his own compositions, one of his major contributions to music is his extensive collections of Hungarian folk music, from which material he often drew in writing his own music. Influences on his earlier music include the works of Richard Strauss and Claude Debussy. He studied in Budapest and, at the age of 26, was appointed to a piano professorship at the Budapest Academy of Music. As a concert pianist, he toured extensively during the 1920s, including a tour of the United States in 1927-1928.

With the rise of fascism in Europe in the 1930s, Bartók and his wife

Top: Béla Bartók. *Bottom:* Hector Berlioz.

emigrated to the United States and settled in New York City. He died there in 1945, in relatively difficult financial straits, just after the end of World War II. He remains one of the most prominent and significant musical figures of the twentieth century.

Bartók's principal orchestral works include two violin concertos, three piano concertos, a viola concerto, and two ballets, *The Wooden Prince* and *The Miraculous Mandarin,* from both of which he extracted concert suites. His *Music for Strings, Percussion and Celesta* is an important study in musical sonorities. An interesting feature of his *Concerto for Orchestra* (1943, revised 1945) is a movement entitled "Game of Pairs," which features a succession of pairs of instruments — bassoons, oboes, clarinets, flutes, and muted trumpets.

LUDWIG VAN BEETHOVEN (1770-1827)

Beethoven was born in Bonn, Germany. His grandfather, a Flemish immigrant (hence the "van," rather than the German "von," in his name), was a prominent Bonn musician. His father, Johann, was also a court musician in Bonn, but of much lower status (he was a court singer, a tenor) than Beethoven's grandfather. Beethoven's father exploited his son as a child prodigy, even falsifying birth records to make Ludwig appear two years younger than he actually was. Beethoven was not the child prodigy that Mozart was, however, and this exploitation only succeeded in giving him emotional traumas which would remain with him for the rest of his life.

Beethoven left Bonn as a young man and went to Vienna, where he had a brief but highly successful career as a concert pianist. His career was cut short, however, by deafness, which began to afflict him in his late twenties, and which almost led him to commit suicide when he was thirty-two. He then turned all his energies to composition, and produced, among many other works, nine symphonies, each of which is a masterpiece.

His first two symphonies are classical, and not so obviously revolutionary in structure or content, and the same is true of his fourth and eighth symphonies. The Third Symphony, however, is conceived on a larger scale. He had planned to call it the *Bonaparte* Symphony, but after Napoleon made himself emperor, Beethoven renamed the work *Eroica*, dedicating it "to the memory of a great man" (i.e.,

Napoleon). The well-known and frequently-performed *Fifth Symphony* is sometimes referred to as the *Fate* Symphony—from the opening theme, which Beethoven said represented Fate knocking at the door. The Sixth Symphony is *programmatic* or meant to evoke a specific feeling. Called the *Pastoral* Symphony, it has five movements, rather than the usual four. The last three are played without pause, which is also unusual. The third movement represents a peasant dance, which is interrupted by a storm; when the storm has spent itself, there follows a song representing the shepherds' thanksgiving. In the Seventh Symphony, each movement is based on a different rhythmic figure; the symphony was later referred to by Wagner as Beethoven's *Dance* Symphony.

The great masterpiece of Beethoven's symphonic output, however, is the massive Ninth Symphony, in which he broke all symphonic precedents by including four vocal soloists and a full choir in the finale. The work is thus frequently referred to as the *Choral* Symphony. The text for the finale is a setting of portions of the great German poet Schiller's *Ode to Joy*, which is a cry for universal brotherhood, a consuming passion of Beethoven's throughout his life.

In addition to his nine symphonic masterworks, Beethoven wrote five piano concertos, a violin concerto, and a triple concerto for violin, cello, and piano.

Beethoven was commissioned to write orchestral music for theatrical productions in Vienna and Budapest; most prominent among Beethoven's contributions to these productions are his music for *Egmont* and the *Coriolan* overture. Also, for his only opera, *Fidelio*, he wrote no fewer than four overtures. The last of these is called *Fidelio* (and is the one that now precedes the opera) but three are called *Leonore*, after the leading female role of the opera.

Today, Beethoven's orchestral works, especially the symphonies, are considered the cornerstone of the repertoire for symphony orchestras throughout the world.

ALBAN BERG (1885-1935)

Berg was born in Vienna, Austria, and was one of the important disciples of the great atonal/dodecaphonic composer Arnold Schoenberg. Berg's concept of Schoenbergian atonality was that it should be used without breaking the continuity of traditional musical style; thus his atonal and twelve-tone works have a distinctive "tonal" sound. Berg's best-known orchestral works are his violin concerto (commissioned by the American violinist Louis Krasner), the *Lyric Suite* (arranged from his own string quartet of that name), and a set of three orchestral pieces. Berg is usually thought of as an opera composer, however, and his two operas, *Wozzeck* and *Lulu*, are masterworks of the twentieth century repertoire. The composer extracted suites from both works.

HECTOR BERLIOZ (1803-1869)

Berlioz was born in La Côte-Saint-André, Isère, in France, the son of a physician. He was the first great orchestrator in music, writing a major book on the subject in 1844, *Treatise on Instrumentation and Modern Orchestration*. His approach to instrumental music was extremely theatrical. His several symphonies are programmatic in nature, with colorful and complex story lines. The first of these was his *Symphonie fantastique*, a symphonic portrayal of a frustrated lover who attempts suicide by a drug overdose, but only fantasizes (hence the title) that he has murdered his beloved, been guillotined for the crime and, in a metaphysical state, discovered his beloved as a participant in a witches' sabbath. Berlioz, like Beethoven, added new instruments to the orchestra, including in this work two harps and the tubular bells. A feature of this symphony is that Berlioz uses a recurring theme in all five movements (the theme representing the beloved of the story), which he called *idée fixe* (fixed idea).

Another important Berlioz symphonic work is his *Harold in Italy*, based on an episode from *Childe Harold's Pilgrimage*, by the English Romantic George Gordon (Lord Byron). This symphony was originally written as a viola concerto for the great string virtuoso Nicolò Paganini, who refused to play it because he considered it not sufficiently difficult. Another popular work, the overture to the second act of his opera *Benvenuto Cellini*, is often played as an orchestral overture with the title *The Roman Carnival Overture*.

Berlioz's gift for orchestration is evidenced in the brilliant orchestral fabric of all of his symphonic works. He had a penchant for larger and larger orchestras, for which he was often caricatured by his contemporaries. An interesting insight into his thinking, tempered with touches of humor, can be enjoyed by reading his book, *Evenings in the Orchestra*.

LEONARD BERNSTEIN (1918-1990)

Leonard Bernstein, born in Láwrence, Massachusetts, is perhaps best known to American audiences as the conductor, for many years, of the New York Philharmonic, and in recent years of orchestras all over the world. His stage works are also well known, including *West Side Story* and *Candide*.

Bernstein's principal orchestral compositions include his three symphonies, entitled, respectively, *Jeremiah* (written in memory of his father), *The Age of Anxiety* (a social commentary based on a poem by W.H. Auden), and the *Kaddish Symphony*, which includes spoken text and chorus, based on the Jewish Kaddish prayer and Bernstein's own words. It is dedicated to the memory of his friend John F. Kennedy, following that President's assassination in 1963.

Bernstein's writing style is traditional in his earlier works, but one finds increasing reference to such twentieth century styles as atonality and dodecaphony (twelve-tone music) in his more recent concert music. His orchestral works are highly dramatic.

GEORGES BIZET (1838-1875)

Georges Bizet, born in Paris, is best known for his opera *Carmen*. Probably his most frequently played orchestral music is the incidental music composed for Daudet's play *The Woman of Arles*. He wrote his *Symphony in C Major* when he was only seventeen, but it was not published until 1935, sixty years after his death. Also, there are two orchestral suites from his opera *Carmen*, both of which have become important parts of the orchestral repertoire.

JOHANNES BRAHMS (1833-1897)

Johannes Brahms, born in Hamburg, Germany, is one of the major symphonic composers of the nineteenth century. His name is often coupled with those of Bach and Beethoven as the "Three B's" of music. Brahms's orchestral music is in the classical mold, but with a romantic sonority and verve. All four of his symphonies are masterworks, as are his other orchestral compositions, including two piano concertos, a violin concerto, a double concerto for violin and cello and two concert overtures. The *Academic Festival Overture* is based on several student songs from German universities, and was written as thanks for an honorary degree awarded him by the University of Breslau. The typical Brahmsian sound is full, rich, and sonorous, and features broad sweeping melodic lines that give all of his orchestral works a universal audience appeal.

Brahms had been an accompanist for the great nineteenth century violinist Joseph Joachim, and the two became close friends. He also had a close personal relationship with Robert and Clara Schumann, particularly with Clara, a leading nineteenth century pianist and the first woman in music to gain international stature. He died of cancer at the age of 63.

BENJAMIN BRITTEN (1913-1976)

Benjamin Britten was born in Lowestoft, Suffolk, in England. He is best known today as an opera composer, following the worldwide success of such works as *Peter Grimes*, *Billy Budd*, *A Midsummer Night's Dream* and *Death in Venice*.

Two of Britten's early orchestral works, the *Simple Symphony* and his set of variations on a theme of the English composer Frank Bridge (Britten's principal teacher), are scored for string orchestra, not the full symphony orchestra. One of his most remarkable works, and one which should be heard, even studied, by anyone seriously interested in symphonic music and the symphony orchestra, is *The Young Person's Guide to the Orchestra*. This work is a set of variations and a fugue based on a theme of the English Baroque composer Henry Purcell. This work features each of the four principal groups of instruments in the orchestra as well as each of the major instruments, in a way that enables the listener to hear each instrument, or family of instruments, quite distinctly and clearly. It is an excellent introduction to the symphony orchestra and all of its component parts.

ANTON BRUCKNER (1824-1896)

Anton Bruckner was born in Ansfelden, Austria, then part of the Austro-Hungarian empire, ruled by the Hapsburgs. Bruckner was best known during his lifetime as an organist. He was, in fact, the Hapsburgs' court organist.

Bruckner's eleven symphonies are reminiscent of the composer's organ training, having full, organ-like sonorities. The sound of a

Top: Benjamin Britten. *Bottom:* **Anton Bruckner.**

Bruckner symphony seems to begin from nothing, with either a single note or a simple interval or chord, and then grows to a mighty climax, often followed by a grand pause of extremely effective silence.

Bruckner's symphonies are heavily romantic in sonority, and are among the great symphonic masterpieces of the orchestral repertoire. They seem to be more popular in Europe than in America, but are fast gaining popularity with American audiences as well.

FRÉDÉRIC CHOPIN (1810-1849)

Born in Poland to a Polish mother and French father, Chopin would become the quintessential composer of piano music during the nineteenth century. His father was a French teacher in a Warsaw high school. Chopin was a child prodigy, making his public debut at the age of eight, at which time he also began to compose music. He did some traveling as a young man, finally settling in Paris when he was 21. In Paris he gave recitals and continued to compose volumes of piano music. In his late twenties he became associated with the author George Sand (Aurore Dudevant), who became his patroness. He was in continuing poor health, eventually contracting tuberculosis, and died in 1849 at the age of 39.

Chopin's only orchestral music consists of two piano concertos and several lesser works for piano and orchestra. These include a set of variations on an aria from the Mozart opera *Don Giovanni*, a fantasia on Polish airs (Chopin remained a Polish nationalist, even though he lived most of his adult life in France), an orchestral rondo and an orchestral *polonaise* (a Polish dance). The orchestration of his piano concertos is often criticized as being weak, but the concertos have remained popular with both performers and audiences.

AARON COPLAND (1900-1990)

Aaron Copland, born in Brooklyn at the beginning of the century, is one of America's leading composers. He studied with Rubin Goldmark in New York, then with Nadia Boulanger in France. Boulanger was an extremely influential teacher of many twentieth century American composers.

Copland's most frequently performed orchestral works were written for the dance, including such masterworks as *Appalachian Spring* (which won him a Pulitzer Prize in 1945), *Rodeo*, and *Billy*

Top: Johannes Brahms. *Bottom:* Aaron Copland.

the Kid. A feature of these works is that they are essentially American in subject matter; his *Lincoln Portrait* and *Fanfare for the Common Man*, both written during the early years of World War II, are especially expressive of American ideals. The Lincoln work features a narrator speaking Lincoln's own words. Other important Copland orchestral works include *Music for the Theater, El Salón México, An Outdoor Overture* and *Quiet City*.

Copland's compositional style is relatively tonal and traditional. A notable exception to this is a 1962 work written for the opening of Lincoln Center in New York. Entitled *Connotations for Orchestra*, it is written in the Schoenbergian twelve-tone method. His music is basically open and stark in sound, making the Copland "sound" readily recognizable. In 1939 he wrote the book *What to Listen For in Music*, which has been widely read and translated into many languages.

CLAUDE DEBUSSY (1862-1918)

Claude Achille Debussy was born in St. Germain-en-Laye. He studied piano with a pupil of Chopin, was educated at the Paris Conservatory, and later spent some time in Russia as music teacher to the children of Madame von Meck, Tchaikovsky's patroness.

Influenced by his exposure to Russian music and to musical exotica at the Paris Exposition of 1889 (especially the *gamelan* music of Bali), Debussy established a musical style which would come to be compared to the literary symbolist school and to the impressionistic school of painting. His musical style soon became identified as *impressionism,* regardless of the fact, as Debussy himself objected, that the label was scarcely an accurate description of his music.

Debussy's style features flowing melodic lines, free rhythmic and metric structures, and the use of non-traditional scale structures such as pentatonic (5-note) and whole-tone scales. His first major orchestral work, a tone poem entitled Prelude to *The Afternoon of a Faun*, is based on Mallarmé's story of the erotic summer dreams of a satyr. (The work is occasionally wrongly interpreted as relating to a *fawn*, rather than *faun*, which gives it a meaning never intended by the composer.) Other major Debussy orchestral works are *La Mer* (The Sea), *Nocturnes* and *Images*.

Debussy died of cancer during the German bombardment of Paris in 1918.

Top: Claude Debussy. *Bottom:* Antonín Dvořák.

FREDERICK DELIUS (1862-1934)

Born Fritz Albert Theodor Delius in Bradford, England, of German parents, Delius was the son of a wealthy export merchant who expected his son to enter the family business. One of the major influences on his style was Edvard Grieg, the Norwegian composer. In his late twenties, after a short stay in Florida cultivating oranges, Delius settled in France, where he remained for the rest of his life. He married the painter Jelka Rosen, but in 1922 was afflicted with a disease (probably syphilis) that left him paralyzed and, eventually, blind. Much of his later work was notated from dictation by his amanuensis, Eric Fenby. Delius's style was romantic, and he excelled in short, programmatic works, such as *On Hearing the First Cuckoo in Spring, North Country Sketches*, and *Brigg Fair*, which are generally nature-inspired.

ANTONÍN DVOŘÁK (1841-1904)

Born in Bohemia (Czechoslovakia today), Dvořák was the son of an innkeeper who wanted his son to be apprenticed to a butcher. His musical talent prevailed, however, and at sixteen he was enrolled in the Prague Organ School. Later he played violin and viola in the orchestra of the Prague State Theater. He won the Austrian State Prize for his Third (E-Flat) Symphony, a prize he would win many more times for his compositions. The composer Brahms was very excited about Dvořák's compositional talents and furthered Dvořák's career by encouraging orchestras to play his music. Dvořák was named Professor of Composition at the Prague Conservatory, and was later awarded an honorary Ph.D. by Cambridge University in England. For a short time he was the artistic director of New York City's National Conservatory, and on an extended visit to a Czech community in Spillville, Iowa, he wrote his very popular *Symphony No. 9* ("From the New World"). He returned to Prague to become artistic director of the Prague Conservatory, and was later honored by the Austro-Hungarian empire, becoming the first musician to be elevated to the Austrian House of Lords. He died in Prague in 1904, at the age of 62.

Dvořák's orchestral music includes nine symphonies; concertos for piano, for violin and for cello; several concert overtures; a set of symphonic variations; two sets of *Slavonic Dances*; and serenades, symphonic poems, marches, and dances.

SIR EDWARD ELGAR (1857-1934)

Born near Worcester, England, Elgar was the son of a church organist, and at an early age studied organ with his father; as a composer, he was self-taught. During his lifetime, Elgar received honorary doctorates from Oxford, Cambridge, Aberdeen, and Leeds Universities in Great Britain and Yale University in the United States. He was named a Knight in 1904 (hence, Sir Edward), appointed Master of the King's Musick in 1924, and made a baronet in 1931.

Elgar's orchestral music includes two symphonies, several concert overtures, concertos for violin and cello, and five orchestral marches, entitled *Pomp and Circumstance*, the first of which is frequently heard at American graduation ceremonies. He also composed a set of orchestral variations on an original theme, called *Enigma Variations*. Each variation relates to a specific person, whom Elgar identifies by initials only.

CÉSAR FRANCK (1822-1890)

Belgian born, the son of a clerk, Franck was a child prodigy, studying at the Liège Conservatory and winning prizes at the ages of nine and twelve for singing and piano respectively. When Franck was thirteen, the family moved to Paris where he studied with Anton Reicha for a time. At fifteen he entered the Paris Conservatory, where he continued to win prizes and honors in piano, composition, and organ. He became one of the finest organists of his time, playing in the well-known Parisian church Sainte Clothilde. At fifty he was named professor of organ at the Paris Conservatory.

His best-known orchestral work is a symphony he did not write until he was sixty-four years old, the *Symphony in D Minor,* which features a beautiful English horn solo in its second movement. He wrote another, little-performed symphony when he was just eighteen, however.

Franck's other orchestral works include a programmatic work entitled *Ce qu'on entend sur la montagne* (What One Hears in the Mountains), a piano concerto, several sets of variations, (including the symphonic variations for piano and orchestra), several tone poems including *Le chasseur maudit* and *Les Djinns*, and a work entitled *Psyché* for orchestra with chorus. His D Minor symphony, however, remains his most frequently played work.

GEORGE GERSHWIN (1898-1937)

Born Jacob Gershvin, Gershwin was the son of a Russian immigrant (who changed his name to Gershvin from Gershowitz). Gershwin was born in Brooklyn, was essentially a self-taught pianist, and began playing the piano in music stores at sixteen. He then took a few lessons from Kilenyi, and later studied harmony with Henry Cowell and Wallingford Riegger. He began his career as a Tin Pan Alley songwriter, and at nineteen wrote "Swanee," which would sell hundreds of thousands of recordings, an astronomical sales figure in those days. With his brother Ira he wrote numerous hit musicals, eventually turning to writing film music on the West Coast. His contributions to concert and operatic stage music include the opera (for an all-black cast) *Porgy and Bess*; a work for piano and jazz band entitled *Rhapsody in Blue* (later orchestrated by his friend Ferde Grofé); a concerto for piano and orchestra; tone poems reflecting his impressions of Paris (*An American in Paris*) and Cuba (*Cuban Overture*); and a relatively unsuccessful second piano rhapsody. Gershwin died of cancer in 1937, at the age of 38, while pursuing a career in film music in Hollywood.

EDVARD GRIEG (1843-1907)

Norwegian-born Grieg, Scandinavia's first important nationalist composer, was actually of Scottish stock, his great-grandfather having emigrated to Norway from Scotland in the late eighteenth century. Grieg studied piano with his mother and, on the recommendation of the great Norwegian violin virtuoso Ole Bull, was sent to study music in Leipzig, Germany, in the tradition of Schumann and Brahms. He also studied for a time with the Danish composer Niels Gade. Shortly thereafter, he married his cousin, the singer Nina Hagerup. His association with the Norwegian writer Henrik Ibsen led to his composing incidental music for Ibsen's nationalistic drama *Peer Gynt*. Grieg spent the latter part of his life in Troldhaugen, near Bergen, on Norway's North Sea coast, where he died of heart disease in 1907, at the age of 64.

Grieg's orchestral music includes a frequently played piano concerto, two orchestral suites taken from the above-mentioned incidental music for Ibsen's *Peer Gynt*, two sets of dances (one arranged from his own four-hand piano works), and a *Lyric Suite*, which is his orchestral version of five of his opus 54 piano pieces.

Top: George Gershwin. *Bottom:* Gustav Mahler.

GEORGE FRIDERIC HANDEL (1685-1759)

Born in Halle, Saxony, Handel was the son of a barber/surgeon and valet who was a servant in an aristocratic house. At the age of seven, Handel was taken by his father to visit an older stepbrother who was also a court valet. Handel, during this visit, found the chapel organ and began to play. He so impressed the duke, who happened to be walking by at the moment, that the duke insisted that the father let the boy study music, something the elder Handel was opposed to. (He wanted his son to study law.) At twelve, Handel held a minor organist's post at Halle Cathedral, and had already begun to write music. He entered the University of Halle to study law when he was eighteen, but quickly turned to music. From Halle he went to Hamburg to play violin in the Hamburg opera orchestra and, while so employed, narrowly escaped death as the result of a hot-headed duel with another musician. He considered the organist's post at nearby Lübeck but, like Bach, turned down the position since it meant marrying the less-than-attractive daughter of the incumbent organist, Buxtehude.

In Hamburg, Handel began to write opera, and he then went to Italy to learn more about Italian opera. He returned to Germany at 23 to become Kapellmeister (music director) for the Prince of Hanover. He took an extended leave to visit England to perform and to have some of his works performed. While he was there, the childless Queen Anne of England died, and the throne was filled by her nearest cousin, the Prince of Hanover, Handel's German patron. Thus Handel remained in England for the remainder of his life. He became well known as a composer of Italian opera and, later, of English-language oratorios, including the great masterpiece *Messiah*. Handel died in 1759, at the age of 74, and was buried with great ceremony in Westminster Abbey in London. He was blind during the last years of his life.

Handel's orchestral music represents only a small portion of his total output, which is primarily vocal, but it includes some frequently performed works. Two of these are orchestral suites he wrote for royal festivities of the new Hanoverian kings, George I and George II. The first, *Water Music*, was written for a royal regatta on the Thames river, and the second, *The Royal Fireworks Music*, was written for a festive occasion featuring fireworks. The story persists that the framework for the fireworks caught fire during the celebration, but the orchestra played bravely on during the ensuing conflagration.

FRANZ JOSEPH HAYDN (1732-1809)

Austrian composer Joseph Haydn is one of the most important composers of orchestral music, particularly symphonies, of the classical era. His contributions to this genre are so important and so extensive that he is often referred to as "the father of the symphony," although he was not the first to write symphonies. His father was a rural wheelwright and his mother a cook. Because of his excellent singing voice, he was sent to Vienna when he was eight, to sing in the choir of St. Stephen's Cathedral. Here he received a good musical education, as well as an excellent general education. He left the choir school in his late teens, did some accompanying in Vienna, and then was taken into the employ of Count Morzin. The Count's court, unfortunately, had financial reversals shortly thereafter, and the court musicians were dismissed. Haydn, through a great stroke of good fortune, was taken on by the wealthy and powerful Esterházy family, and remained with them (soon thereafter as Kapellmeister, or music director) for the remainder of his life.

Haydn was a masterful composer of symphonies, writing 104 such works. Symphonies 82-87 were written for the court orchestra of the French King, Louis XVI, and his Austrian Hapsburg Queen, Marie Antoinette, and are now referred to the *Paris* symphonies. His symphonies 93-104—the final twelve—were written on two trips Haydn made to England (then ruled by the German-born Hanoverian kings), and are now referred to as either the *London* Symphonies or the *Salomon* Symphonies (after the London concertmaster/impresario who was responsible for bringing Haydn to England). While in England, Haydn was given an honorary doctorate by Oxford University, an honor (and title) he prized highly. He retired in Vienna, and died there in 1809, at the age of 77, while Napoleon's French troops were in occupation of the city.

Haydn also wrote a *sinfonia concertante* (a symphony featuring several solo instruments), and concertos for violin, cello, trumpet, flute, horn, and harpsichord, as well as several multiple-instrument concertos.

PAUL HINDEMITH (1895-1963)

German-born, and the son of a house painter, Hindemith turned early to music, taking violin lessons at the age of nine. He entered Frankfurt's Hoch Conservatory at the age of twelve, studying there for ten years. During this time he wrote a great deal of music. At twenty, he became concertmaster (first chair, first violinist) of the Frankfurt opera and then formed a string quartet, the Amar Quartet, which would soon become quite famous. In this quartet, however, he played the viola, not the violin. He taught at the Berlin Mu-sikhochschule until he came into conflict with Nazi ideologies. He went to Turkey, where he accepted the job of reorganizing that country's public school music program. By the late 1930s he was teaching at the Tanglewood Summer Music Festival in Massachusetts. In 1940, he was named to the music faculty of Yale University in Connecticut, and also lectured at Harvard. He became an American citizen in 1947. Shortly after the war, however, he returned to Europe—not to his native Germany, but to Switzerland—to teach at the University of Zürich. He died in Switzerland in 1963, at the age of 68.

Hindemith wrote a number of ensemble works that he called either *Kammermusik* (chamber music) or *Konzertmusik* (concert music). Of the so-called chamber works, most are concertos for small orchestra and piano, violin, cello, viola, organ or viola d'amore (a predecessor of the violin family of instruments). Of the so-called concert music series, the most frequently performed is a 1930 work for strings and brass. He also wrote full concertos for organ, cello, horn, clarinet, and violin, and orchestral concertos (featuring several orchestral instruments).

Two sets of orchestral variations are also important: a set of variations for piano and string orchestra, *The Four Temperaments*, and a work that goes far beyond simple theme and variation technique, the *Symphonic Metamorphoses*, based on themes taken from the work of the nineteenth century composer Carl Maria von Weber. Hindemith's orchestral output exhibits a great deal of variety and encompasses numerous forms and compositional techniques.

GUSTAV HOLST (1874-1934)

Born in England, Holst studied organ with his father. When he was nineteen, he entered the Royal College of Music in London where he studied composition. He was music director at St. Paul's School for Girls from 1905 and at London's Morley College from 1907 until his death, and also taught composition at the Royal College of Music. He toured the United States, lecturing in various cities. He was extremely interested in exotic subjects, especially Hindu and Oriental music, as well as in English folklore.

Holst's best-known work is an orchestral suite, *The Planets*, whose seven movements have far more to do with astrology than with astronomy. Another of his orchestral works which has gained some popularity is his *Somerset Rhapsody*. There are two works, *St. Paul's Suite* and *Brook Green Suite*, for string orchestra. Other Holst orchestral works include *Beni Mora*, *Egdon Heath*, and a *Japanese Suite*.

CHARLES IVES (1874-1954)

Connecticut-born Charles Ives was the son of a Danbury bandmaster, who taught his son music in such a way as to encourage young Ives to turn to bitonality (music in two different keys simultaneously) and avant-garde compositional techniques. Ives went to Yale, where he studied (but did not enjoy) traditional music with Horatio Parker. Incidentally, Ives was also an excellent athlete while at Yale, especially in baseball. After leaving Yale, Ives was a church organist for a time in New York, then teamed up with a friend named Julian Myrick to found an insurance company (a new concept in those days), and amassed a multimillion dollar fortune in a very few years. He continued to write music as an avocation, allowing himself all sorts of experimentation in his composing. His music features many direct quotes from American folk music, but a great deal of it is written in a avant-garde style that discouraged its performance and acceptance until the 1950s, nearly half a century after it was written.

Ives' *First Symphony*, relatively traditional in style, was written while he was still at Yale. The *Second Symphony*, in five movements, is a bit more complex, and the *Third Symphony* is a programmatic work, *The Camp Meeting*. The *Fourth Symphony* adds to the final movement a chorus singing an American folk hymn. A fifth Ives symphony, the *Holidays Symphony*, features movements relating to the American holidays—Washington's Birthday, Decoration Day, July 4th and Thanksgiving. (These four movements were written at different times.) A major Ives orchestral work is a three-movement composition, *Three Places in New England*, which is, in part, highly polytonal.

Ives wrote a number of shorter orchestral pieces, many of them extremely avant-garde, such as *The Unanswered Question*, which features a solo trumpet, a group of flutes and a small string orchestra all playing different things at different times. Ives's *Third Symphony* won a Pulitzer Prize in 1946.

FRANZ LISZT (1811-1886)

Hungarian-born Franz Liszt, the son of an official in the service of Prince Nicholas Esterházy (Haydn's patron), studied piano with his father, and was soon recognized as a child prodigy. The family moved to Vienna, where Liszt studied with Czerny and Salieri. Liszt eventually settled in Paris with his family, later beginning a series of brilliant tours as a concert pianist, which would take him to every corner of Europe and skyrocket him to enormous fame.

In his late thirties, Liszt gave up his concert career to take a position as music director in the ducal court in Weimar, where he began to compose his symphonic poems. He himself contrived this genre, essentially a single-movement programmatic work. He later entered a monastery to become an abbot and remained in the monastery for the rest of his life, but continued to travel from time to time.

Liszt's orchestral music is dominated by his two piano concertos, two programmatic symphonies (the *Faust* and *Dante* symphonies), and thirteen symphonic poems. The symphonic poems involve such subjects as *Hamlet, Orpheus* and *Tasso*, but the best known is the third, entitled *Les Préludes*, based on a poem by Lamartine.

GUSTAV MAHLER (1860-1911)

Born in Kalischt (now Kaliste) Bohemia, today part of Czechoslovakia, but then part of the Austro-Hungarian Empire, Mahler was the son of a tavern keeper. After music lessons with local musicians, he was enrolled in the Vienna Conservatory, where he abandoned his piano studies in favor of composition. Mahler's major activity in music, in addition to composing, was as a highly-successful conductor, especially of opera, holding posts in Prague, Budapest, Vienna and New York, where he was conductor of both the Metropolitan Opera and the New York Philharmonic. He died in Austria in his early fifties.

Although Mahler composed only during the summer, when he was not conducting, he wrote nine major symphonies and began a tenth. His first symphony, subtitled *The Titan,* features a funeral march based on the familiar canon *Frere Jacques.* In his second, third and fourth symphonies, Mahler followed Beethoven's lead, adding voices to the symphonic structure. In his second symphony, subtitled *The*

Resurrection, he included one of his own songs from his collection *The Youth's Magic Horn, Urlicht,* and a setting of Klopstock's *Auferstehung (Resurrection).* In his third symphony he included a setting of a text from Nietzche's *Thus Spake Zarathustra,* as well as another of his *Wunderhorn Songs, Es sungen drei Engel.* In his fourth symphony he included still another of his *Wunderhorn* songs, *Des Himmliche Leben.* The fifth, sixth and seventh symphonies are again purely instrumental, the sixth, subtitled *Hammerschlag,* including three hammer strokes, representing to Mahler his daughter's death, his heart condition and his own death. He again added voices in his massive eighth symphony, subtitled *Symphony of a Thousand,* with eight soloists, a boychoir and a mixed chorus, the first part a setting of the Latin sacred text *Come, Holy Spirit* and the second part a setting of the final scene of Goethe's *Faust.* The ninth symphony is his last complete symphony and his tenth had only two movements completed at his death.

FELIX MENDELSSOHN (BARTHOLDY) (1809-1847)

Born in Hamburg, Germany, the son of a banker, and the grandson of the Jewish philosopher, Moses Mendelssohn, Mendelssohn was raised in Berlin, where his family moved when he was a small boy. He was a gifted child and was given the best mucical training at home, but not exploited as a child prodigy as young Mozart had been.

His first successful composition was written at sixteen, an overture to a production of Shakespeare's *Midsummer Night's Dream.* He became a relatively successful concert pianist, and developed into one of music's first important conductors, conducting, at 20, the performance of J.S. Bach's *St. Matthew Passion,* which brought about the revival of Bach's music. He also conducted a series of historical concerts at Leipzig's Gewandhaus concert hall, including music from Bach to Beethoven and contemporary pieces from his own generation.

He was also a principal founder of the Leipzig Conservatory at the age of 30. He was widely honored, receiving an honorary Ph.D. from the University of Leipzig and was a favorite house guest of Queen Victoria and Prince Albert in England.

The sudden death of his elder (by four years) sister Fanny, led to a stroke, followed by several more, and he died in 1847 at the age of 38.

As a teenager, Mendelssohn wrote a dozen symphonies and several concertos. As a mature composer he wrote five symphonies, including the *Rhenish, Italian, Scottish* and *Reformation* symphonies. He composed two piano concertos and a very popular violin concerto, as well as the overtures *The Hebrides (Fingal's Cave), Die Schoene Melusine* and *Ruy Blas,* plus a tone poem *Calm Sea and Prosperous Voyage* and his incidental music to *Midsummer Night's Dream.*

WOLFGANG AMADEUS MOZART (1756-1791)

Mozart was one of the most remarkable musical geniuses ever to have lived. He was concertizing as a harpsichordist and violinist when he was just five years old, and by the time he was eight he had written the first of his approximately 50 symphonies. Despite a brilliant concert career as a child and teenager, however, he was unable to fit into the mold of the patronage system which dominated music during the eighteenth century, and lived on commissions and gifts from friends. He married and had two sons, but was never in financial control of his life.

Mozart was the son of a well-known violinist and violin teacher, Leopold Mozart, who guided his son's life and career as a young man, but was unable to control and guide him after his move to Vienna and his subsequent marriage. Eventually, after writing some of the greatest music ever composed, Mozart died a pauper's death at 35 and was buried in an unmarked grave. The mystery surrounding his early death is still, two centuries later, unresolved.

Mozart composed 21 piano concertos, five violin concertos, four horn concertos, one of the first clarinet concertos (a new instrument in Mozart's day), and several multiple concertos, including a popular work for flute and harp. He also wrote a great deal of so-called "occasional" music, such as his frequently-performed serenade *Eine kleine Nachtmusik (A Little Night Music)*, numerous dances, and a number of works he called divertimentos, cassations, and serenades —even a tongue-in-cheek work he called *A Musical Joke*. A great composer by all standards, Mozart, despite his tragically short life, was one of music's giants.

MODEST MUSSORGSKY (1839-1881)

One of the great Russian nationalist composers of the nineteenth century, Mussorgsky was first taught piano by his mother, an amateur pianist. At 13 he was enrolled in the cadet school of the Russian Imperial Guard, and he later served with that force. He left the military, however, turning to music, and studied with Balakirev. When his family's fortunes were reversed, he became a government clerk. He waged a lifelong battle with alcoholism. He became associated with that group of Russian nationalist composers known as the "Mighty Handful" (occasionally referred to as the "Russian Five"), which also included Rimsky-Korsakov, Borodin, Balakirev, and Cui.

Mussorgsky's major nationalistic works, however, were written not for the orchestra, but for piano and for the operatic stage. *Pictures at an Exhibition* is a set of programmatic piano pieces dealing with an art exhibition. It has been orchestrated many times, but perhaps most successfully by the French composer Maurice Ravel, and is now frequently performed as an orchestral work. *Boris Godunov* is his great Russian nationalist opera, and is most frequently heard in a version adapted and orchestrated by his colleague Rimsky-Korsakov.

Mussorgsky was forced out of government service at 41 because of his excessive drinking. His alcoholism killed him just a year later.

Much of Mussorgsky's orchestral music is taken from his operas, including *Boris Godunov*, and *Khovanchina*. He is best known as an orchestral composer, however, by the very popular orchestral tone poem, *Night on Bald Mountain*.

KRZYSZTOF PENDERECKI (b. 1933)

Polish composer Penderecki (pronounced Pen-de-ret-ski) is an active composer on the international scene. He received his musical training at the conservatory in Cracow, Poland, and startled the musical world by entering a composition contest, submitting, under false names, three of his own works and taking all three prizes. He continues to lecture widely on music throughout the world. His early music was quite avant-garde, featuring tone-clusters and frequent startling dissonances. In the late 1960s he mellowed somewhat and began to write more traditionally, yet without compromising his own style.

Penderecki has written two operas and several major choral works, as well as a violin concerto, a cello concerto, and a concerto-like work he calls *Sonata for Cello and Orchestra*. One of his best-known works is a remarkable piece for 52 strings dedicated to the victims of the atomic bombing of Japan at the close of World War II and entitled *Threnody for the Victims of Hiroshima*. His works also include a composition for two orchestras entitled *Emanations*, a capriccio for violin and orchestra, a work for 48 strings entitled *Polymorphia*, and a canon for strings and two magnetic tapes. He wrote his first symphony in 1973; his more traditional second symphony, the *Christmas Symphony*, features the melody of the popular Christmas carol "Silent Night". Penderecki continues to rank as one of the major composers of the second half of the twentieth century.

SERGEI PROKOFIEV (1891-1953)

Born in Czarist Russia, Prokofiev took his first piano lessons from his mother, who was an amateur pianist. At thirteen he entered the St. Petersburg Conservatory, where he studied with Rimsky-Korsakov. He also became a brilliant concert pianist and had an extremely successful concert career, traveling throughout the world. He dabbled in his composition with the style of neo-classicism, especially with his first symphony, written in 1917, and later subtitled "The Classical Symphony." However, later his less-than-traditional writing led him to a falling out with the Soviet censors, especially with Lenin's successor, Josef Stalin. He was required to publicly recant his musical "sins" and, except for a few trips abroad, he remained in Russia until his death at 61, after the end of World War II. (Ironically, he died almost the exact day that his nemesis, Stalin, died).

Prokofiev's orchestral works include, in addition to the symphony mentioned above, six more symphonies, a sinfonietta, and a sinfonia concertante featuring a solo cello. A concert pianist, Prokofiev wrote five piano concertos, including one (No. 4) for the left hand alone, and two violin concertos. He composed seven ballets, extracting one or more orchestral suites from each of them; the suites from *Romeo and Juliet* and *Cinderella* are perhaps the most popular. He wrote music for at least eight films, including *Alexander Nevsky*, *Lieutenant Kijé*, and *Ivan the Terrible*. His narrated orchestral work for children, *Peter and the Wolf*, remains one of his most popular and endearing works.

Top: Sergei Prokofiev. *Bottom:* Maurice Ravel.

SERGEI RACHMANINOV (1873-1943)

One of the great pianists of the late nineteenth and early twentieth centuries, Rachmaninov was born to wealthy Russian parents who were quite musical. Both his father and his grandfather were good amateur pianists. The family suffered financial reverses, but Rachmaninov was educated properly in St. Petersburg and Moscow. Tchaikovsky heard him play and praised his talents, so Rachmaninov turned to a concert career and became one of his generation's leading concert pianists. He performed worldwide and, at the same time, pursued an equally successful career as a composer. He left Russia when the Soviets took over, never to return to his homeland. During the mid-1930s he moved to the United States, living for a time in New York. He finally settled in Los Angeles, where he died in his Beverly Hills home in 1943, as the Second World War raged in Europe. He was 69 years old when he died, and was lauded as one of the great pianists of the twentieth century, as well as one of this century's leading composers.

His four piano concertos are of major importance. The second of these has been particularly popular in the concert world and is played with great frequency. Another extremely popular Rachmaninov orchestral work is a set of variations for piano and orchestra (a kind of piano concerto) based on a simple theme by the great nineteenth century violinist, Paganini, which Rachmaninov called *Rhapsody on a Theme of Paganini*. He wrote three symphonies, all of which remain in the orchestral repertoire to varying degrees, and a set of symphonic dances.

MAURICE RAVEL (1875-1937)

Ravel was born in Basque country, in the area of the Pyrenees mountains which separate France and Spain. His father was a Swiss engineer. The family moved to Paris when Ravel was just an infant, so his environment was not rural Basque, but cosmopolitan Parisian. He began piano and theory lessons at seven and eleven years of age, respectively, and when he was fourteen entered the Paris Conservatory to study piano. He also studied composition with Gabriel Fauré. Some of the music he wrote during these years is still played, including his frequently-performed *Pavane for a Dead Princess*. He studied in Rome, having won the coveted Prix de Rome (Rome Prize), which was competitively awarded to young French composers for musical study in that city. The delicacy of much of Ravel's orchestration has led many to compare his works for orchestra to those of Debussy, which are sometimes called "impressionistic." There is also a neo-classical element to Ravel's music, however, even though his piano music shares Debussy's keen interest in tone color.

Ravel became one of the modern era's great orchestrators, along with Rimsky-Korsakov and Richard Strauss. In 1921 he was awarded an honorary Ph.D. by Oxford University, the first of many honors he would receive during his lifetime. In 1932 Ravel was in an automobile accident. The concussion he received from that accident led to a degenerative brain disease in his later life, causing a lack of muscular coordination and bouts of aphasia. He died, after an unsuccessful brain operation, in 1937, at the age of 62.

Although Ravel never wrote a symphony, his orchestral work is remarkable. One of his most popular works, reflecting his gift for orchestration as well as recalling his Basque heritage, is *Bolero*.

Ravel also wrote two piano concertos. One is an excellent concerto for the left hand, which he wrote on commission for the concert pianist Wittgenstein, who lost his right hand during World War I. His hauntingly beautiful ballet *Daphnis and Chloé* features the celesta and a wordless chorus. Also reflecting Ravel's Basque heritage is his very popular *Rapsodie espagnole* (*Spanish Rhapsody*). His *Mother Goose Suite* (later expanded into a ballet) is also popular, as is his (perhaps satirical) tour de force entitled *La Valse*.

NIKOLAI RIMSKY-KORSAKOV (1844-1908)

Rimsky-Korsakov was one of the leading composers of Czarist (pre-Soviet) Russia, a major teacher and, with Ravel, Berlioz, and Richard Strauss, one of music's great orchestrators. He was sent, at the age of twelve, from his country home to the Royal Naval Academy at St. Petersburg. He graduated from the academy at the age of 18. He had piano lessons as a child and his musical education was influenced by Balakirev. Both Rimsky-Korsakov and Balakirev would later become part of that group of Russian nationalist composers known as the "Mighty Handful," occasionally referred to as the "Russian Five".

An important musical work of his, perhaps inspired by his naval voyages, is his symphonic suite based on the Arabian Nights which he named for the story-teller herself, *Sheherazade*. His *Capriccio es-*

pagnol also may have been inspired by a visit of his ship to Spain during his naval career.

Returning to Russia, Rimsky-Korsakov was appointed professor of
composition at the St. Petersburg Conservatory, where he remained
until his death in 1908 at the age of 63. He became quite famous as an
outstanding teacher during those years and wrote a major treatise on
orchestration, which complemented the one Berlioz had written
earlier in the nineteenth century. Rimsky-Korsakov's naval career finally ended in 1873, after he assumed his professorial position at the
conservatory, but he continued to inspect navy bands for some time
thereafter. He did some conducting, both at home and abroad, and
remained active as a teacher and as a leader of the Russian nationalist
movement.

Rimsky-Korsakov's orchestral works also include three symphonies, of which the second, subtitled *Antar*, is occasionally performed. His most frequently heard works include *Sheherazade* and
the *Capriccio espagnol*, already mentioned. *The Russian Easter
Overture* is probably the most nationalistic of his works, and is highly
representative of an aspect of his orchestration technique in which
solo instruments are frequently featured.

CAMILLE SAINT-SAËNS (1835-1921)

Raised by a widowed mother and a great-aunt (who gave him his
first piano lessons), Saint-Saëns was one of France's most important
composers of the nineteenth century. He was playing the piano in
public at the age of five and composing at the age of seven. He entered the Paris Conservatory in his mid-teens, studying organ and
composition.

Saint-Saëns became an organ virtuoso, playing the organ in the
Madeleine church in Paris. He then devoted himself entirely to composition, teaching only an occasional piano student. He was one of
the founders of the French National Society of Music, which was established to encourage the performance of music by French composers. He married, had two sons who died in infancy, and later lived
apart (but never divorced) from his wife (he lived to be 86, she to be
95).

Saint-Saëns was much honored during his lifetime, being awarded
the highest honor of the French Legion of Honor, as well as an honorary Ph.D. from Cambridge University in England. He traveled widely
and occasionally performed, one of his "feats" being the playing of

entire Wagner music dramas at the piano (he was an avid Wagner fan). He gave up his love of German music, however, when the Germans invaded France during World War I (he was nearly 80 when the war began). He died a few years after the war, in 1921.

Saint-Saëns wrote three symphonies, of which the third, the so-called "Organ Symphony", is best known. This symphony is in two principal sections and features, in honor of the great pianist (and later organist) Franz Liszt, a prominent organ part and a prominent piano part for four hands. Saint-Saëns also wrote a number of concertos, including two for cello, three for violin and five for piano. The piano concertos are extremely difficult to play (he himself was an excellent concert pianist). He wrote several non-concerto works for piano and orchestra as well as the frequently performed tone poem, *Danse macabre*. A popular work is the humorous *Carnival of the Animals*. He would not allow this work to be played until after his death. Although frequently played by a large orchestra today, it was conceived by Saint-Saëns as a chamber work for a small group of instruments and two pianos.

ARNOLD SCHOENBERG (1874-1951)

The Viennese-born Schoenberg is one of the most important composers of the modern era, because his compositional explorations of harmony led him beyond tonal music, first into music that was atonal (literally, without a tonal, or key, center)—Schoenberg preferred the term "pantonal"—and eventually to his "dodecaphonic," or twelve-tone, method, in which all twelve notes of the chromatic scale were to have equal importance.

Schoenberg began his working career as a bank clerk in Vienna at the age of sixteen after his father's sudden death. He continued, however, to study music, notably the cello, which he played very well. He was also an excellent painter. His early compositions are quite traditional. His first break with tonality came just before the beginning of World War I, with his first atonal works, which were written for piano. In 1910 he was named professor of composition at the Vienna Academy, at which time he wrote his theory textbook *Harmonielehre*. A textbook on traditional harmonic practices, it is still used today. He also traveled to major European cities to conduct his works, receiving mixed response. His 1912 work *Pierrot lunaire*, for example, was almost booed off the stage in Berlin.

Schoenberg established a society in Vienna for the furthering and performance of new music. He renounced his Jewish faith in his late teens, but with the onslaught of Hitler's fascism and the ensuing holocaust, he publicly reaffirmed his faith. Shortly after that he emigrated to the United States, where he joined the music faculties of both U.C.L.A. and U.S.C. in Los Angeles. He became an American citizen in 1941, just before America's entry into World War II. He lived the rest of his life in the United States, suffering a heart attack in 1946, and steadily declining in health until his death in 1951 at the age of 76.

Schoenberg's orchestral works include concertos for piano and violin, two chamber symphonies, an orchestral suite entitled *Five Pieces for Orchestra*, a tone poem based on *Pélleas and Mélisande*, the subject of Debussy's great opera, a suite for string orchestra and an atonal work entitled *Variations for Orchestra*. His last major tonal work before his move to atonality was *Verklärte Nacht* (*Transfigured Night*). It was conceived as chamber music (for string sextet) and later scored by him for string orchestra.

FRANZ SCHUBERT (1797-1828)

Schubert ranks among composers as the quintessential songwriter. He wrote more than 700 songs, or *Lieder*. The son of a schoolmaster, Schubert tried his hand at this profession in his late teens, but hated it and turned to music, spending the rest of his short life (he died at 31) living on the largesse of family and friends. He was given violin lessons at eight, and at eleven was accepted as a Vienna Choirboy, as a result of which he received an excellent music education as well as a fine general education. He composed his first orchestral works while still attending the choir school.

During the last decade of his life, he and his circle of friends often had what they called "Schubertiads" on various evenings or weekends, during which they would play, sing and enjoy Schubert's newly-composed works, few of which were published or performed professionally during his lifetime. He earned very little money from his works, and had no musical patron. He certainly would have lived out his life in poverty, had it not been for the generosity of his friends. He succumbed to typhus at the age of 31, but he had been frail and ailing for most of his life. He was quite short (5' 2") and very much overweight (his friends called him "the sponge"), as well as extremely myopic (he wore very thick eyeglasses for most of his life).

Despite all of these physical and personal problems, he was one of the most lyrical and creative musical geniuses of all time.

Schubert's orchestral works include ten symphonies, of which the most frequently played are the 8th (in B Minor), of which he completed only two of the planned four movements and which was dubbed the *Unfinished*; and his final symphony, "The Great C Major" Symphony, so nicknamed because there was an earlier Schubert symphony in C Major, which then came to be known as "The Little". In addition to these symphonic works, Schubert wrote a number of overtures, some ballet music (for the play *Rosamunde*), and other short works. Curiously, he wrote no concertos, except for a work for violin and orchestra which he called *Concertstück* (*Concert Piece*). Although Schubert stands out as the great songwriter of music, his orchestral works, particularly his late symphonies, justify his position as an important orchestral composer as well.

ROBERT SCHUMANN (1810-1856)

The son of a Saxon bookseller who had mental problems which his son probably inherited, Schumann displayed both musical and literary talent as a boy, and pursued both of these vocations during his career. At the age of eighteen he went to Leipzig, where he studied piano with the great piano teacher Friedrich Wieck and eventually fell in love with Wieck's talented daughter, Clara, whom he would later marry. (Clara was to become the first female performer and composer of international fame in the history of music.) The Schumanns had seven children, one of whom, Ferdinand, a gifted poet, died of consumption in his late teens.

Most of the music written by Schumann before his marriage to Clara was piano music. After he married Clara, he turned first to writing songs, and eventually to orchestral music.

In addition to his composing, Schumann was active as a writer and was one of the first important figures of nineteenth century music journalism. He edited a music magazine (still published today) entitled *Neue Zeitschrift für Musik* (*New Journal of Music*) which presented new composers, such as Chopin and Brahms, and commented on new works and on performances.

Schumann suffered from mental problems all his life, and he attempted suicide at the age of 44. After this, he was institutionalized for the last two years of his life, and never fully regained his mental faculties. He died in 1856, at the age of 46.

Schumann's orchestral music includes four symphonies, the first subtitled *Spring* and the third *Rhenish* (from the Rhine). His symphonies are quite lyrical—as one might expect from a song writer. He wrote a piano concerto which has become one of the most popular works in the concerto repertoire, and concertos for cello and violin. The overture to his opera *Genoveva* is occasionally programmed as an orchestral work, and he wrote three theatrical overtures, *The Bride of Messina* (Schiller), *Hermann and Dorothea* (Goethe) and *Julius Caesar* (Shakespeare).

ALEXANDER SCRIABIN (1872-1915)

The only child of an aristocratic Russian family, Scriabin was the son of a lawyer. His mother was a gifted pianist, but died just a year after Alexander's birth. His father spent his life in the Russian consular service in Turkey, and Alexander was left in Russia to be raised by two aunts and a grandmother.

Scriabin became an excellent concert pianist, studying at the Moscow Conservatory, where he was a classmate of Rachmaninov. He concertized widely, continued to compose, and was for a time on the faculty of the Moscow Conservatory. He turned to mysticism later in his life and also became involved with the concept of the perception of color in music. He died in 1915, in the early years of World War I, at the age of 43.

Although the majority of Scriabin's works are for piano, he wrote several important orchestral works, including five symphonies. The composer's subtitles to the last three of these symphonies are indicative of the mystical side of his personality: No. 3 is *The Divine Poem*, No. 4 *The Poem of Ecstasy*, and No. 5 *Prometheus, the Poem of Fire*. These are brilliantly orchestrated, featuring the ringing sound of high brass, and are rich in harmonic structure and sonority. Scriabin developed a special device to project colors during the performance of *Prometheus*, an "instrument" he called the *chromelodeon*. This instrument was part of his continuing conviction that color was an essential part of music—that each key or tonality represented a different color in the spectrum, the concept of Chromesthesia.

DMITRI SHOSTAKOVICH (1906-1975)

Born in St. Petersburg (Leningrad today), Shostakovich entered the conservatory there in 1919 at the age of 13, studying piano and composition. Success came quickly to him: his graduation piece from the conservatory, his *First Symphony*, was highly praised at its 1926 premiere in Leningrad. This symphony was performed in Berlin under Bruno Walter the following year, and in Philadelphia under Leopold Stokowski in 1928. Shostakovich's first nine symphonies were written within the next twenty years, the second entitled *To October* (for the tenth anniversary of the Russian Revolution). The Seventh is often referred to as the *Leningrad* Symphony, since it was written during the German siege of Leningrad during World War II. One of his major symphonic works is the monumental *Fifth Symphony*, which he wrote in 1937.

In 1948 Stalin decreed that Soviet composers should renounce what he perceived as avant-garde compositional techniques, identified by him as "formalism," and Shostakovich did not write another symphony for five years—until after the death of Stalin. His Eleventh and Twelfth symphonies were nationalistic, the Eleventh called *To the Year 1905,* the year of the first Russian Revolution. The Twelfth is dedicated to Lenin and to the year 1917, the year of the second Russian Revolution. Far more controversial, however, was Shostakovich's Thirteenth Symphony, entitled "Babi Yar" after the site of a massacre of Jews by the Soviet military during World War II. This symphony is based on five poems overtly or implicitly critical of shortcomings of the Soviet state.

When he was 60, Shostakovich developed a severe heart condition and acute arthritis. He died in 1975, just before his 69th birthday. Both his son Maxim and his grandson Dmitri, a conductor and pianist respectively, left Russia after Shostakovich's death, emigrating to the United States.

In addition to his fifteen symphonies, Shostakovich wrote a number of other orchestral works, including suites from his opera *The Nose* and his ballet *The Age of Gold*. The latter is an extremely popular work in the orchestral repertoire, especially the polka from this suite. He wrote several other ballets, two violin concertos, two piano concertos and two cello concertos.

JEAN SIBELIUS (1865-1957)

A strong Finnish nationalist composer, Sibelius was very much involved with Finnish mythology, and many of his major works express these interests.

Born into a Swedish-speaking family in Finland, Sibelius changed his given name from Johan to Jean, but is occasionally also referred to as Jan. His father, a doctor, died of cholera when Jean was only two years old. Sibelius was educated in a Finnish-speaking public school and studied law for a year at Helsinki University before turning to music as a career, studying in Berlin, Leipzig, and Vienna.

Returning to Finland after his musical studies in Germany and Austria, Sibelius was unable to acquire a major teaching position in music, and turned to private teaching instead. He was able also to earn money from his composing and was later given a small pension by the Finnish state. Mounting debts and heavy drinking contributed to his inability to acquire a major position. His creative life all but ended in the 1920s, although he lived until 1957.

The orchestral works of Sibelius are frequently oriented toward Finnish nationalism, as with his tone poems *En Saga* and *Tapiola*, the suite entitled *Lemminkäis-sarja* (which includes the frequently-played tone poem *The Swan of Tuonela*), and his popular nationalist work entitled *Finlandia*.

Sibelius is known as a major symphonist, having written seven symphonies. His orchestral style is occasionally referred to as "lapidary," or constructed from layers of sound. He also wrote a violin concerto and a number of shorter, often programmatic, orchestral works.

BEDŘICH SMETANA (1824-1884)

Smetana, one of music's first important nationalist composers, was born in Bohemia (today a part of Czechoslovakia), the son of a German-speaking brewer in the service of Count Waldstein (one of Beethoven's patrons was a member of this aristocratic family). Smetana's father was an amateur violinist and Bedřich was his eleventh child, but the first son to survive infancy.

A child prodigy in music, Smetana was playing the piano in concert at the age of six. He went to Prague to study music when he was fourteen, where he heard Liszt play and was inspired to become a professional musician. He once wrote that he hoped to become a "Liszt in technique and a Mozart in composition."

He opened his own music institute when he was twenty-four, but it was not successful. Subsequently, he moved to Sweden and opened a similar school in Göteborg which was, on the contrary, extremely successful. He returned to Prague twelve years later, in 1861. He became active at this time as a nationalist, writing nationalistic operas and collecting folk music.

In 1874 he began to lose his hearing and, within a year or two, his mental health began to deteriorate as well. He was eventually committed to an asylum, where he died in the spring of 1884, shortly after his sixtieth birthday.

Smetana wrote primarily chamber music and piano music. His few important orchestral works include a set of nationalistic tone poems entitled *Má vlast* (*My Country*), which includes the frequently performed tone poem *Vltava* (*Moldau*), Bohemia's principal river. His *Triumph Symphony* features folk music as its thematic material.

JOHANN STRAUSS, JR. (1825-1899)

A son of the Viennese violinist and composer Johann Strauss, Sr., Strauss Jr. became the most widely acclaimed of the several members of the Strauss family who were active in music. Although the waltz had been popular in Vienna and most of Europe since before the beginning of the nineteenth century, the Strauss family, Johann Jr. especially, elevated this dance to a more sophisticated musical level. As a result, the waltz generally, and Strauss waltzes especially, attained a popularity worldwide far beyond any the dance had previously known. Strauss's father discouraged his son from entering music as a profession, preferring that he should become a banker, even though young Johann displayed a great deal of talent. Johann studied music secretly, however, and eventually began the serious study of music, finally to be acclaimed internationally as the "waltz king," following in his father's footsteps and followed in turn by his brothers Josef and Eduard, both excellent musicians.

Strauss's orchestral music consists primarily of dance forms, most notably waltzes, polkas, and quadrilles. His most famous waltz is probably the frequently performed *On The Beautiful Blue Danube*.

RICHARD STRAUSS (1864-1949)

The son of a famous Munich horn player (and no relation to the Viennese Strauss dynasty), Richard Strauss was a gifted child and was active musically from the age of four. He performed from the age of fourteen as a violinist in his father's orchestra. Strauss was quite active as a composer in his late teens and early twenties, during which time he also acquired a passion for conducting. He eventually became a conductor of world class.

At the outbreak of World War II Strauss was 75 and decided to remain in Nazi Germany as a conductor. This decision was widely misunderstood, and Strauss fell out of favor with many audiences after the war. He went into voluntary exile in Switzerland, but was reconciled with the musical world in 1947, just two years before his death, with an invitation to attend a Strauss festival in London.

Strauss was one of music's greatest orchestrators, which is to say he had a natural talent for writing for each instrument or combination of instruments of the orchestra in such a way as to display them at their best.

Strauss's first major works were a horn concerto he wrote for his father and the symphonic poem *Don Juan*. He is best known orchestrally for his masterful tone poems. Tone poems are single-movement, programmatic symphonic works, a form originally established by the Hungarian pianist Franz Liszt. Strauss's tone poems are portrayals of literary characters—*Don Juan, Macbeth* and *Don Quixote*; philosophical in nature—*Thus Spoke Zarathustra (Also Sprach Zarathustra)* and *Death and Transfiguration (Tod und Verklärung)*; geographical/pictorial—*Aus Italien (From Italy)* and *Eine Alpensinfonie (An Alpine Symphony)*; and even autobiographical—*Ein Heldenleben (Hero's Life)* and *Symphonia Domestica (Domestic Symphony)*. Strauss was equally well known as an opera and song composer.

IGOR STRAVINSKY (1882-1971)

The son of a famous Russian opera singer, Fyodor Stravinsky, Stravinsky grew up in the cultured city of St. Petersburg in a house always filled with music. He was given piano lessons as a child, but was guided into the study of law and spent eight terms at St. Petersburg University studying law before he turned to music. One of his student friends was Vladimir Rimsky-Korsakov, son of the great

Top: Dmitri Shostakovich. *Bottom:* Richard Strauss.

Russian composer, and through their friendship Stravinsky eventually came to study instrumentation with the elder Rimsky-Korsakov, an acknowledged master of orchestration and instrumentation.

Stravinsky's first orchestral work, *Feu d'artifice* (*Fireworks*), was written to celebrate the wedding of Rimsky-Korsakov's daughter (Rimsky-Korsakov died without hearing it). This work was heard by the ballet impresario Serge Diaghilev, who liked it so much that he commissioned Stravinsky to compose for his ballet company. The first work he wrote for it was *The Firebird*, soon followed by *Petrushka* and *The Rite of Spring*, the latter work so advanced that it caused riots at its 1913 Paris premiere.

Stravinsky spent the years of the First World War in Switzerland, after which he moved to France. He was forced to move again when the Germans occupied France in 1940. He settled in the United States, became an American citizen, and spent his last years in Southern California and New York.

In addition to the ballets mentioned above, Stravinsky also wrote a work entitled *Symphonies of Wind Instruments*, a symphony for 23 wind instruments, plus four other symphonies, *the Symphony in E flat, the Symphony in C*, the *Symphony in Three Movements*, and the *Symphony of Psalms*, which eliminates the upper strings but includes a choir singing psalm settings. He also wrote a violin concerto, a concerto for chamber orchestra (*Dumbarton Oaks*) and a concerto for clarinet and jazz band (the *Ebony Concerto*) for the American clarinetist Woody Herman. Stravinsky often wrote orchestral music on commission, including a circus polka, which was written for elephants of the Barnum and Bailey circus.

Stravinsky ranks as one of the giants of twentieth century music, and his orchestral music is an important part of his creative output.

PETER TCHAIKOVSKY (1840-1893)

The son of a mining engineer, Tchaikovsky exhibited musical talent as a child and was given piano lessons. As a young man in St. Petersburg, he spent a year at the School of Jurisprudence, after which he worked for a time as a clerk at the Ministry of Justice. He left that post after three years to turn to the study of music, spending several years at the conservatory headed by Anton Rubinstein. After graduating from the conservatory, Tchaikovsky moved to Moscow, where he was hired to teach harmony at the Moscow Conservatory. Here he wrote the first of his six symphonies.

Shortly thereafter, Tchaikovsky turned to the composition of ballets, which were fast becoming a major art form in Russia. He wrote some of his best music for ballet, including such masterpieces as *Swan Lake* and *Sleeping Beauty*.

Shortly before a disastrous marriage (he was a homosexual) Tchaikovsky acquired the patronage of a wealthy widow, Nadezhda von Meck, who admired his music and offered him a generous stipend to support his composing, with the unusual proviso that they never meet socially. Tchaikovsky died at 53 of what was thought to be typhus from drinking tainted water, but recent research suggests that he may have committed suicide by taking poison.

Tchaikovsky is one of the most popular composers of orchestral music, perhaps because of his remarkable talent for creating beautiful melodies. He occasionally lamented his weakness in the area of musical structure, however, once commenting that his music seemed to "show the seams," meaning, perhaps, that he was not comfortable with his ability to connect one section of a movement with another.

Tchaikovsky wrote six symphonies, the first subtitled *Winter Daydreams*, the second *Little Russian*, the third *Polish*, and the sixth *Pathétique*. He also wrote several symphonic poems, including a *Romeo and Juliet* fantasy and a *Francesca da Rimini* fantasy after Dante. One of Tchaikovsky's most popular orchestral works is the *1812 Overture*, written to commemorate the defeat of Napoleon in Russia in that year. This overture features a musical "war" between the French and Russian national anthems, complete with the sounds of cannons and church bells.

RALPH VAUGHAN WILLIAMS (1872-1958)

Vaughan Williams was the youngest of three children of an English clergyman who died when Vaughan Williams was only three. The family included prominent lawyers and judges, and was connected with the biologist Charles Darwin. Vaughan Williams had piano and theory lessons as a child, and studied violin and viola in secondary school. He spent two years at the Royal College of Music in London, and three years at Cambridge, where he took degrees in both music and history. He later studied with Bruch in Berlin and Ravel in Paris.

Vaughan Williams became involved with folk music quite early in his career and spent a good deal of time collecting and publishing English folk songs. Especially important is his collection of English hymn tunes. After World War I he joined the faculty of the Royal College of Music as a teacher of composition, a position in which he influenced and guided a number of important younger English composers.

His wife of 53 years died in 1951, and he remarried at the age of 81. He was in good health, other than being somewhat deaf, and continued to travel and lecture both in Europe and in the United States until his death in 1958 at the age of 85.

Of Vaughan Williams's orchestral works, several of the earlier are nationalist in character as a result of his interest in folk music. These include the *Norfolk Rhapsody*, and a composition he called a symphonic impression, entitled *In the Fen Country*. More characteristic of Vaughan Williams's mature works, rather than the quotation of actual folksongs, is his assimilation, like Bartók, of elements of the folksongs of his country into his own personal style. His interest in the music of earlier English composers is evidenced in his *Fantasia on a Theme by Thomas Tallis*. He composed nine symphonies, including several programmatic symphonies, such as his first, *A Sea Symphony*, which includes solo and choral voices, with text by the American poet Walt Whitman. A particularly popular orchestral work of Vaughan Williams is his *Fantasia on Greensleeves*, based on two familiar English folk songs.

Occasionally his orchestral works have extra-musical origins, such as his Seventh Symphony, *Sinfonia Antartica*, which was developed from music written for a film about the British exploration of Antarctica. Vaughan Williams's music is essentially traditional, and was not influenced by the more extreme new musical styles of the twentieth century, such as atonality, serial music and electronic music.

ANTONIO VIVALDI (1678-1741)

Vivaldi was the eldest of six children of a violinist who was a member of the orchestra of St. Mark's Cathedral in Venice. Vivaldi himself decided as a young teenager to become a priest. He entered the seminary at 15, and was ordained as a priest at 25. He soon became known as *il prete rosso* ("The Red Priest") because of his red hair. He did not remain active as a priest for very long, however, because of a continuing asthmatic condition. Since he was unable to fulfill the active duties of a priest, Vivaldi turned to music, and was named master of violin at the Pietà, a Venetian school for homeless girls. He began

Top: **Igor Stravinsky.** *Bottom:* Ralph Vaughan Williams.

to write solo concertos, and became the first great master of this genre, eventually writing more than five hundred concertos for nearly every instrument in the eighteenth century orchestra.

He did not get along well with the administration and staff at the Pietà, so he began to travel. He turned to opera during this period and wrote a number of operas, few of which are known today. He also performed during this period, playing for aristocrats, kings, and popes. He was a poor manager of his personal finances, however, and spent the last years of his life in near-poverty in Vienna, where he died at the age of 63.

Vivaldi's orchestral works are made up primarily of the more than five hundred solo and ensemble concertos he wrote. Four of these concertos were given titles and grouped together as a collection entitled *The Four Seasons*, the four concertos being named "Spring," "Summer," "Autumn," and "Winter," respectively.

RICHARD WAGNER (1813-1883)

Wagner was the youngest of nine children born to a police chief who died a year after Richard was born. His mother's second husband was Ludwig Geyer, an actor who also painted and wrote poetry. Some historians believe that Geyer was Wagner's real father. Wagner was obsessed with literature as a young student, but Beethoven's symphonies inspired him to turn to music as a career. He wrote several orchestral overtures and a symphony while he was studying music at the University of Leipzig.

Wagner's principal compositional activity, however, was in the field of opera, which he transformed into a totally new concept of music and theater. He called this concept "music drama"; it essentially discarded the aria/recitative structure of traditional opera. His monumental *Ring of the Nibelungs*, which deals with the mythological history of the northern European peoples, comprises four separate operas and meant to be performed on four successive evenings. Although performances of *The Ring* in its entirety are becoming somewhat more frequent than in the past, such an endeavor is a formidable undertaking for all involved. Individual performances, particularly of the second opera, *Die Walküre* (*The Valkyrie*), are much more common.

Wagner was active as an opera director in Riga (Latvia) and Dresden (Saxony). He was exiled to Switzerland from Dresden after he became involved in the political uprising of 1848. After his return from Switzerland he went to Bavaria, where he obtained the unlimited patronage of the young King Ludwig II. He eventually designed and built a theater for the express purpose of producing his music dramas, in the town of Bayreuth, north of the Bavarian capital, Munich.

Wagner's early orchestral overtures and his single symphony are rarely played, but excerpts from his music dramas, especially the preludes and overtures, are frequently programmed as orchestral works. Particularly popular are the overtures to *Rienzi, Lohengrin, The Mastersingers* and *The Flying Dutchman*. His use of brass instruments is particularly effective. He even went so far as to have a special tuba designed, so that he could have an entire family of these brass instruments.

Despite a great deal of controversy concerning the man himself and his writings on non-musical subjects, Wagner's music remains, the work of a remarkable composer and important innovator.

ANTON WEBERN (1883-1945)

Viennese-born Webern was the son of a well-to-do minor aristocratic family. He went to school in Klagenfurt, then enrolled at the University of Vienna to study with the noted musicologist Guido Adler. He soon became a disciple of the atonalist/serialist Arnold Schoenberg and became one of the principal exponents of the Schoenberg method. He was also active as a conductor. The onslaught of the Nazi occupation of Austria and the beginning of World War II brought Webern's musical activity to a close and he spent the remainder of his life in the town of Mittersill, near Salzburg, where he was accidentally shot by an American military policeman shortly after the end of the war.

Webern's orchestral music is deeply rooted in Schoenbergian atonality and serialism, as mentioned above. His later works reflect a preoccupation with total serialization—i.e., the serialization of dynamics, instruments, etc., as well as pitches. He also wrote a number of extremely short pieces, and is occasionally referred to as a miniaturist. The movements of some of his works last less than a minute.

His orchestral music includes a Passacaglia (a Baroque form built over a bass line), and several works titled according to the number of movements in each, such as *Five Movements, Six Pieces* and *Eight Fragments*. He wrote a single symphony (just nine minutes in length) and a set of orchestral variations.

His orchestral style is highly structured and has a clean, spare sound. A particular aspect of his style is his pointillism, in which single musical pitches are presented almost "in isolation"—a single note played by only one instrument may, at some moments, constitute the entire orchestral texture. These moments may be flanked by silence, or they may multiply, sometimes very rapidly, creating bursts, or "points," of sound. Webern's orchestral work, although not extensive, constitutes an important body of twentieth century instrumental music.

* * *

Haydn's "Farewell" Symphony No. 45, in which one by one in the final movement each musician blew out his candle and exited with his instrument, prompted Prince Esterhazy to grant leave to his musicians.

* * *

A beggar once approached Mozart for money. Mozart sat down at the next coffee house and wrote a Minuet for him. He then instructed the beggar to take the music to his publisher, who gave the beggar a small sum of money.

* * *

On Beethoven—
"He is an utterly untamed personality, not entirely in the wrong if he finds the world detestable, but does not thereby make it more enjoyable for himself or others."—Goethe

* * *

Dvorak had an affinity for pigeons and locomotives. He developed a new hobby in New York—steamships.

* * *

Stravinsky was almost charged with breaking an ordinance in 1944 for his new orchestration of the "Star Spangled Banner." It was against the law to "tamper with" the national anthem.

* * *

Chapter 8

NOW WHO'S AFRAID
OF THE SYMPHONY ORCHESTRA?

We have many opportunities to listen to great music today—in the concert hall and through the media of recordings, videos and television. Standards of excellence prevail. While certain large cities remain the center of cultural activity, the decentralization of musical life in the United States is also a reality. Qualified professionals abound.

The following pages offer a basic record-library list, suggestions for further reading, and a lighthearted summary of concert etiquette. The authors hope that this book has helped you acquire a better understanding of the music and musicians that make up the world of the symphony orchestra. This knowledge, of course, is helpful, but let us remember that the *music itself,* the *sound* of music, is *most* important. So, wherever you live, enjoy listening and support "your" symphony orchestra!

A BASIC REPERTOIRE LIST

BACH, JOHANN SEBASTIAN
    Six Brandenburg Concertos
    Four Orchestral Suites

BARBER, SAMUEL
    Adagio for Strings
    Symphony No. 1
    The School for Scandal Overture
    Piano Concerto

BARTOK, BELA
    Concerto for Orchestra
    Music for Strings, Percussion and Celesta
    Piano Concerto No. 3

131

BEETHOVEN, LUDWIG VAN
Symphony No. 1
Symphony No. 2
Symphony No. 3 ("Eroica")
Symphony No. 4
Symphony No. 5
Symphony No. 6 ("Pastoral")
Symphony No. 7
Symphony No. 8
Symphony No. 9 ("Choral")
Piano Concerto No. 1
Piano Concerto No. 2
Piano Concerto No. 3
Piano Concerto No. 4
Piano Concerto No. 5 ("Emperor")
Violin Concerto
Leonore Overture No. 3
Egmont Overture
Coriolan Overture

BERG, ALBAN
Violin Concerto
Three Pieces for Orchestra

BERIO, LUCIANO
Sinfonia

BERLIOZ, HECTOR
Symphonie fantastique
Harold in Italy
Roman Carnival Overture
Benvenuto Cellini Overture

BERNSTEIN, LEONARD
Symphony No. 1 ("Jeremiah")
Symphony No. 3 ("Kaddish")
Symphonic Dances from *West Side Story*

BIZET, GEORGES
Symphony in C Major
L'Arlesienne Suites
Carmen Suites

BLOCH, ERNEST
Schelomo

BORODIN, ALEXANDER
Polovetsian Dances from *Prince Igor*
On the Steppes of Central Asia
Symphony No. 2

BRAHMS, JOHANNES
Symphony No. 1
Symphony No. 2
Symphony No. 3
Symphony No. 4
Academic Festival Overture
Tragic Overture
Variations on a Theme of Haydn
Double Concerto (for violin and cello)

BRITTEN, BENJAMIN
The Young Person's Guide to the Orchestra

BRUCH, MAX
Violin Concerto No. 1

BRUCKNER, ANTON
Symphony No. 4 ("Romantic")
Symphony No. 7

CAGE, JOHN
Concerto for Prepared Piano

CHÁVEZ, CARLOS
Sinfonía india

CHOPIN, FRÉDÉRIC
Piano Concerto No. 1
Piano Concerto No. 2

COPLAND, AARON
Appalachian Spring
Rodeo
Lincoln Portrait
Billy the Kid

DEBUSSY, CLAUDE
Prelude to *The Afternoon of a Faun*
La Mer
Nocturnes
Images

DELIUS, FREDERICK
Brigg Fair

DOHNANYI, ERNÖ
Variations on a Nursery Song

DUKAS, PAUL
The Sorcerer's Apprentice

DVOŘÁK, ANTONÍN
Symphony No. 7
Symphony No. 8
Symphony No. 9 ("From the New World")
Slavonic Dances

ELGAR, EDWARD
Cockaigne Overture
Enigma Variations

FRANCK, CÉSAR
Symphony in D Minor

GERSHWIN, GEORGE
Piano Concerto in F
Rhapsody in Blue
An American in Paris

GOLDMARK, KARL
Rustic Wedding Symphony

GRIEG, EDVARD
Piano Concerto
Peer Gynt Suites

GROFÉ, FERDE
Grand Canyon Suite

HANDEL, GEORGE FREDERIC
Water Music
Music for the Royal Fireworks

HAYDN, FRANZ JOSEPH
The "Paris" Symphonies Nos. 82-87
The "London" Symphonies Nos. 93-104

HINDEMITH, PAUL
Mathis der Maler
Symphonic Metamorphoses on Themes of Carl Maria
    von Weber

HOLST, GUSTAV
The Planets

d'INDY, VINCENT
Symphony on a French Mountain Air

IVES, CHARLES
Three Places in New England
The "Holidays" Symphony
Symphony No. 2
Symphony No. 3 ("Camp Meeting")

KABALEVSKY, DMITRI
The Comedians
Violin Concerto

KHATCHATURIAN, ARAM
Gayne Ballet Suite
Masquerade Suite

LALO, EDOUARD
Symphonie espagnole

LISZT, FRANZ
Piano Concerto No. 1
Piano Concerto No. 2
Les Préludes
"Faust" Symphony

MAHLER, GUSTAV
Symphony No. 1 ("Titan")
Symphony No. 2 ("Resurrection")
Symphony No. 3
Symphony No. 4
Symphony No. 5
Symphony No. 6
Symphony No. 7
Symphony No. 8 ("Symphony of a Thousand")
Symphony No. 9
Das Lied von der Erde ("The Song of the Earth")

MENDELSSOHN, FELIX
Symphony No. 3 ("Scottish")
Symphony No. 4 ("Italian")
Violin Concerto in E Minor
Hebrides Overture ("Fingal's Cave")
Midsummer Night's Dream

MILHAUD, DARIUS
La Création du monde

MOZART, WOLFGANG AMADEUS
Symphony No. 35 ("Haffner")
Symphony No. 36 ("Linz")
Symphony No. 38 ("Prague")
Symphony No. 39
Symphony No. 40
Symphony No. 41 ("Jupiter")
Piano Concertos

MUSSORGSKY, MODEST
Pictures at an Exhibition
A Night on Bald Mountain

PENDERECKI, KRZYSZTOF
Threnody for the Victims of Hiroshima

PROKOFIEV, SERGEI
Peter and the Wolf
Lt. Kijé Suite
Symphony No. 1 ("Classical")
Symphony No. 5

RACHMANINOV, SERGEI
Piano Concerto No. 2
Rhapsody on a Theme of Paganini
Symphony No. 2

RAVEL, MAURICE
Daphnis et Chloé
Bolero
Piano Concerto for the Left Hand
Rhapsodie Espagnole

RESPIGHI, OTTORINO
The Pines of Rome
The Fountains of Rome
Roman Festivals

RIMSKY-KORSAKOV, NICOLAI
Sheherazade
Capriccio espagnol
Russian Easter Overture

ROSSINI, GIOACCHINO
The Barber of Seville Overture
William Tell Overture

SCHOENBERG, ARNOLD
Verklärte Nacht (Transfigured Night)
Five Orchestral Pieces

SCHUBERT, FRANZ
Symphony No. 8 ("Unfinished")
Symphony No. 9 ("Great C Major")

SCHUMANN, ROBERT
Piano Concerto
Symphony No. 1 ("Spring")
Symphony No. 3 ("Rhenish")

SHOSTAKOVICH, DMITRI
Symphony No. 1
Symphony No. 5
Symphony No. 7 ("Leningrad")
The Age of Gold Suite

SIBELIUS, JEAN
Finlandia
Symphony No. 2
Symphony No. 5

SMETANA, BEDŘICH
The Moldau
The Bartered Bride Overture

STRAUSS, RICHARD
Don Juan
Death and Transfiguration
Till Eulenspiegel
Don Quixote
Also sprach Zarathustra
Ein Heldenleben

STRAVINSKY, IGOR
The Firebird
Petrushka
The Rite of Spring

TCHAIKOVSKY, PETER
Symphony No. 4
Symphony No. 5
Symphony No. 6 ("Pathétique")
Nutcracker
Swan Lake
Sleeping Beauty

VAUGHAN WILLIAMS, RALPH
Symphony No. 1 ("A Sea Symphony")
Fantasia on "Greensleeves"
Fantasia on a Theme by Thomas Tallis

VIVALDI, ANTONIO
The Four Seasons

WAGNER, RICHARD
Rienzi Overture
Die Meistersinger Overture
Prelude to Act III of Lohengrin

Siegfried Idyll
Ride of the Valkyries
Tannhäuser Overture

WEBERN, ANTON
Six Pieces for Orchestra

SUGGESTIONS FOR FURTHER READING

Biographical Bibliography

Bach: Geiringer, Karl: *Johann Sebastian Bach: The Culmination of an Era*, London: Oxford, 1966.
Barber: Broder, Nathan: *Samuel Barber*, New York: G.Schirmer, 1954.
Bartók: Stevens, Halsey: *The Life and Music of Béla Bartók*, New York: Oxford University Press, 1953.
Beethoven: Burk, John, *The Life and Works of Beethoven*, New York: Random House, 1943.
Berg: Redlich, Hans: *Alban Berg: The Man and His Music*, New York: Abelard-Schuman, 1957.
Berlioz: Barzun, Jacques: *Berlioz and His Century*, New York: Columbia University Press, 1969.
Bernstein: Cone, Molly: *Leonard Bernstein*, New York: Thomas Y. Crowell, 1970.
Bizet: Curtiss, Mina: *Bizet and His World*, New York: Knopf, 1958.
Brahms: Gál, Hans: *Johannes Brahms, Trans. Joseph Stein*, London: Severn House, 1975.
Britten: Holst, Imogen: *Britten*, London: Faber, 1980.
Bruckner: Doernberg, Erwin: *The Life and Symphonies of Anton Bruckner*, New York: Dover, 1968.
Chopin: Gavoty, Bernard: *Frédéric Chopin, trans. Martin Sokolinsky*, New York: Scribner, 1977.
Copland: Berger, Arthur: *Aaron Copland*, New York: Oxford, 1953. Dickinson, Peter: *Copland at 75*, Musical Times CXVI, 1975.
Debussy: Nichols, Roger: *Debussy*, London: Oxford, 1973.
Delius: Fenby, Eric: *Delius*, London: Faber, 1971.
Dvořák: Clapham, John: *Dvořák*, New York: Norton, 1979.
Elgar: Parrott, Ian: *Elgar*, London: Dent, 1971.
Franck: Davies, Laurence: *Franck*, London: Dent, 1973.
Gershwin: Ewen, David, *A Journey to Greatness*, New York: Allen, 1956.
Grieg: Horton, John: *Grieg*, London: Dent, 1974.
Handel: Lang, Paul Henry: *G.F. Handel*, New York: Norton, 1977.
Haydn: Landon, H.C. Robbins: *Haydn*, London: Faber, 1972.
Hindemith: Skelton, Geoffrey: *Paul Hindemith: The Man Behind The Music*, London: Crescendo, 1975.
Holst: Holst, Imogen: *The Music of Gustav Holst*, London: Oxford University Press, 1986.

Ives: Hitchcock, H.Wiley: *Ives*, London: Oxford University Press, 1977.

Liszt: Perényi, Eleanor: *Liszt*, New York: Weidenfeld and Nicolson, 1975.

MacDowell: Gilman, Lawrence: *Edward MacDowell: A Study*, London: Da Capo, 1969.

Mahler: Wiesmann, Sigrid ed.: *Gustav Mahler in Vienna*. New York: Rizzoli: International Publications, 1976.

Mendelssohn: Selden-Goth G.: *Felix Mendelssohn: Letters*. New York: Vienna House, 1973.

Mozart: Einstein, Alfred: *Mozart: his Character, his Work*, New York: Oxford University Press, 1968.

Keys, Ivor: *Mozart: His Life in Music*, London: Granada, London, 1980.

Mussorgsky: Serov, Victor: *Modeste Mussorgsky*, New York: Funk and Wagnalls, 1968.

Penderecki: Robinson, Ray: *Krzysztof Penderecki: A Guide to His Works* Princeton, N.J.: Prestige Publications, 1983.

Prokofiev: Seroff, Victor: *Sergei Prokoviev: A Soviet Tragedy*, New York: Taplinger, 1979.

Rachmaninov: Norris, Geoffrey: *Rakhmaninov*, London: Dent, 1976.

Ravel: Nichols, Roger: *Ravel*, London: Dent, 1977.

Rimsky-Korsakov: Abraham, Gerald: *Rimsky-Korsakov: A Short Biography*, London: A.M.S. Press, 1976.

Saint-Saëns: Harding, James: *Saint-Saëns and His Circle*, London: Chapman/Hall, 1965.

Schoenberg: Rosen, Charles: *Arnold Schoenberg*, New York: Princeton, 1981.

Schubert: Brown, Maurice: *Schubert: A Critical Biography*, London: Da Capo, 1977.

Schumann: Chissell, Joan: *Schumann*, London: Dent, 1977.

Scriabin: Macdonald, Hugh: *Scriabin*, London: Oxford University Press, 1978.

Shostakovich: Norris, Geoffrey: *Shostakovich: The Man and His Music*, London: Boyars, 1982.

Sibelius: Layton, Robert: *Sibelius and His World*, New York: Viking, 1970.

Smetana: Clapham, John: *Smetana*, London: Dent, 1972.

Strauss, Johann: Wechsberg, Joseph: *The Waltz Emperors*, London: Putnam, 1973.

Strauss, Richard: Kennedy, Michael: *Richard Strauss*, London: Dent, 1983.

Stravinsky: Routh, Francis: *Stravinsky*, London: Dent, 1975.

Tchaikovsky: Volkoff, Vladimir: *Tchaikovsky: A Self-Portrait*, Boston: Crescendo, 1974.

Vaughan Williams: Vaughan Williams, Ursula: *RVW: A Biography*, London: Oxford University Press, 1964.

Vivaldi: Talbot, Michael: *Vivaldi*, London: Dent, 1984.

Wagner: Newman, Ernest: *The Life of Richard Wagner*, London: Cassell, 1976.

Webern: Moldenhauer, Hans: Anton von Webern: *Chronicle of His Life and Works*, New York: Random House, 1978.

General Bibliography

Apel, Willi. *The Harvard Dictionary of Music*. 2d rev.ed. Cambridge: Harvard, 1969.

Applebaum, Samuel and others. *The Way They Play*. Vol. 1-13 Neptune City, N.J.: Paganiniana.

Austin, William. *Music in the Twentieth Century*. New York: Norton, 1966.

Baines, Anthony, ed. *Musical Instruments through the Ages*. New York: Walker, 1975.

Bekker, Paul. *The Orchestra*. New York: Norton, 1963.

Bernstein, Leonard. *The Joy of Music*. New York: Simon and Schuster, 1980.

Bernstein, Leonard. *The Unanswered Question*. Cambridge: Harvard, 1981.

Blume, Friedrich. *Classic and Romantic Music*. New York: Norton, 1970.

Camner, James. *Great Composers in Historic Photographs*. New York: Dover, 1981.

Camner, James. *Great Conductors in Historic Photographs*. New York: Dover, 1982.

Carse, Adam. *The History of Orchestration*. New York: Dover, 1964.

Chase, Gilbert. *America's Music from the Pilgrims to the Present*. 2d rev. ed. New York: McGraw-Hill, 1966.

Copland, Aaron. *Copland on Music*. New York: Norton, 1963.

Copland, Aaron. *The New Music 1900-1960*. New York: Norton, 1968.

Cowell, Henry. *American Composers on American Music*. New York: Ungar, 1962.

Dallin, Leon. *Listener's Guide to Musical Understanding*. 6th ed. 1986.

Deyries, Bernard. *The Story of Music in Cartoon*. New York: Arco, 1983.

Ewen, David. *Complete Book of Classical Music*. Englewood Cliffs, N.J.: Prentice-Hall, 1968.

Ewen, David. *The World of 20th Century Music*. Englewood Cliffs, N.J.: Prentice-Hall, 1968.

Feather, Leonard. *The Book of Jazz*. New York: Dell, 1976.

Feather, Leonard. *The Encyclopedia of Jazz*. rev. ed. New York: Horizon, 1960.

Ferguson, Donald. *Masterworks of the Orchestral Repertoire*. Minneapolis: University of Minnesota Press, 1954.

Grout, Donald. *A History of Western Music*. rev. ed. New York: Norton, 1973.

Hindemith, Paul. *A Composer's World*. Cambridge: Harvard, 1952.

Kalischer, A.C. *Beethoven's Letters*. New York: Dover, 1972.

Lang, Paul Henry and Nathan Broder, eds. *Contemporary Music in Europe: A Comprehensive Survey*. New York: Norton, 1967.

Longyear, Rey M. *Nineteenth-Century Romanticism in Music*. 2d ed. Englewood Cliffs, N.J.: Prentice-Hall, 1973.

Machlis, Joseph. *Introduction to Contemporary Music*. New York: Norton, 1961.

Marcuse, Sybil. *Musical Instruments: A Comprehensive Dictionary*. New York: Norton, 1975.

Miller, Hugh M. *Introduction to Music*. New York: Harper and Row. 2d ed. 1978.

Moore, Douglas. *A Guide to Musical Styles*. New York: Norton, 1962.

Palisca, Claude V. *Baroque Music*. Englewood Cliffs, N.J.: Prentice-Hall, 1968.

Pauly, Reinhard G. *Music in the Classic Period*. 2d ed. Englewood Cliffs, N.J.: Prentice Hall, 1973.

Prendergast, Roy M. *Film Music: A Neglected Art*. New York: Norton, 1977.

Previn, André, ed. *Orchestra*. Garden City, New York: Doubleday, 1979.

Randolph, David. *This is Music*. New York: Mentor Books, 1965.

Ratner, Leonard G. *Music: The Listener's Art*. 2d ed. New York: McGraw-Hill, 1966.

Sachs, Harvey. *Toscanini*. New York: Da Capo Press, 1978.

Sadie, Stanley, ed. *A History of Western Music*. rev. ed. New York: Norton, 1973.

Salzman, Eric. *Twentieth-Century Music: An Introduction*. 2d ed. Englewood Cliffs, N.J.: Prentice-Hall, 1974.

Schonberg, Harold. *The Great Conductors*. New York: Simon and
    Schuster, 1967.
Schonberg, Harold. *The Lives of the Great Composers*. New York: Si-
    mon and Schuster, 1967.
Schwartz, Elliott. *Electronic Music: A Listener's Guide*. New York:
    Praeger, 1973.
Scholes, Percy A. *Concise Oxford Dictionary of Music*. Edited by J.G.
    Ward. 2d ed. New York: Oxford, 1964.
Sessions, Roger. *Questions About Music*. New York: Norton, 1971.
Schuller, Gunther. *Early Jazz: Its Roots and Musical Development*.
    New York: Oxford, 1968.
Simpson, Robert, ed. *The Symphony: Haydn to Dvořák*. Vol. 1. New
    York: Penguin Books, 1978.
Simpson, Robert, ed. *The Symphony: Elgar to the Present Day*. Vol. 2.
    Baltimore: Penguin Books, 1975.
Thompson, Oscar. *The International Cyclopedia of Music and Mu-
    sicians*. Edited by Bruce Boble. 10th rev. ed. New York: Dodd,
    Mead, 1975.
Veinus, Abraham. *The Concerto*. New York: Dover, 1964.
Walter, Bruno. *Of Music and Music Making*. New York: W.W. Norton,
    1960.

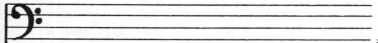

CONCERT ETIQUETTE*

Though all audience members are part of the species called *Homo sapiens*, when placed in a large room for the express purpose of attentive listening these individuals often exhibit amazing traits. The following descriptions may seem frightening, unreal, almost more mythical than the unicorn; but rest assured that at least one member of each species named has been sighted. Ask yourself whether you haven't observed several of them in attendance at one of your concerts.

Any resemblance to real persons, living or deceased, is strictly intentional. We have endeavored to balance all references and comments to offend both sexes equally. In keeping with current lawsuit practices, only the names have been changed to protect the guilty.

THE COMMENTATOR (*bigus mouthus*)—This supposedly learned creature inhabits nearly every concert hall. Many variations of the species exist, all sharing one common trait—the inability to let a single chord pass, nay even one note of melody, without a verbal description of same to someone nearby. They often travel in packs, feeding one another's egos. Volume levels range from barely audible (maddening!) to one dynamic level above the music being played. The species is readily identifiable by such comments as, "Wow, did you notice that countermelody?" Of course, you didn't because of all the people around you making similar comments.

---

*Reprinted by permission from *The Instrumentalist* (April 1987)—"Concert Etiquette" by David C. Hunt and Ron Berg.

THE RUSTLER (*figetus programmus*)—Waits until the house lights have gone out to read the concert program. Straining to see what is printed, he turns the pages constantly, weaving and bobbing, until finally some light is shed on the subject. Unaware that it is now intermission, he has overlooked the first half of the performance. At times this type may bring along his own lighting. This is not actually used to assist reading, but to assist others in identifying him.

TIMEKEEPERS (*beepus beepus*)—Plural. Never travels alone. Arrives in colonies with others of like bent who meet secretly before the performance to synchronize digital wrist-watch alarms. Each attendee sets his alarm to go off precisely on the hour, then each one sets the time on his watch slightly different from anyone else in the group. Have also been known to cause whiplash and embarrassing spontaneous hand-clapping by awakened Mr. ZZzzz's in attendance.

THE COUGH DROP KID (*wrapus cellaphanus*)—This type always carries cough drops, hard candies, or chewing gum in brittle wrappers. In an emergency, such as nothing to do but listen to the performance, one of these soothing objects can be pulled out quickly and unwrapped sllooowwwwly, so as not to disturb others.

THE ACCOMPANIST (*bandus one-manus*) Almost always a former percussionist or vocalist. Thrives in college music department audiences. Often brings own set of instruments including pencils, pens, spiral notebooks, paperclips, and a comb. Extremely creative in using chairs, arms, legs, and fingertips to create striking ostinato rhythmic accompaniments for every piece performed. Occasionally found humming in parallel major thirds above the melody. Enjoys active participation, with or without audience acknowledgement.

MR. ZZzzz (*dozus perfectus or sleepii beauteous*)—This species takes on many forms and can inhabit the body of nearly anyone. Causes of behavior range from fatigue to boredom. Observable characteristics include comatose stare, chin-dropping, stretching, fidgeting, and resting head on companion's shoulder. Audible characteristics include sighing between movements, grotesque yawning, and pronounced snoring.

THE ENTHUSIAST (*clappus too-soonus*)—Not known to be malevolent, merely misguided. Truly enjoys the performance and wishes to express appreciation, but is not sure at which point to applaud: end of the piece? after each movement? after each soloist? It's *sooo* confusing! Doesn't want these grand musicians to think he didn't appreciate how great they were, so applauds at every lull in performance, no matter how brief.

MRS. BO-JANGLES (*jewelrii danglus*)—A colleague of The Accompanist. Appears with an entire percussion section draped around her neck, wrists, and ankles. Jewelry is most often coordinated to insure the availability of a full range of octaves and timbres. Light, tinkling bracelet descant is matched with low brass melodies, while rattling of heavy metal necklaces is reserved for flute soliloquies.

While variations and mutations of each of the above-named species exist in concert halls, it is wise to recognize that the exact evolutionary direction of those described remains under investigation by music sociologists. Though no definitive study has yet been published, it is theorized in some circles that the intervention of some powerful force, such as education, may alter the behavior of concert audiences of the next century.

ABOUT THE AUTHORS

Lucas Drew is Chairman and Professor of Double Bass in the Department of Instrumental Performance at the University of Miami and Principal Bass of the Philharmonic Orchestra of Florida, which also performs for the Miami Opera. He has performed with many of the world's great musicians, including Stravinsky, Stokowski, Villa-Lobos, Maderna, Boulanger, Sevitzky, Lombard, Henze, and Copland. He is soloist on recordings for the Coronet, Spectrum, and Golden Crest labels and has appeared on the NBC Today Show, BBC-TV, NPR, and PBS. Summer guest-faculty and performance appointments include the Brevard Music Center, Dartmouth College, Indiana University, Stetson University, and many recitals and workshops throughout the U.S. and Europe. He is founder and Artistic Director of the Highlands (N.C.) Chamber Music Festival. He is among the artists included in Samuel Applebaum's *The Way They Play.* Dr. Drew served as editor for the International Society of Bassists, 1974-1982, and as President of the American String Teachers Association from 1982-1984. His more than 50 published editions of music for solo double bass, chamber music, and string orchestra are played throughout the world.

Raymond Barr is presently the Chairman of the Musicology Department of the University of Miami School of Music in Coral Gables, Florida. Educated at Penn State, Carnegie-Mellon and the University of Wisconsin, Dr. Barr has done doctoral and Post-Doctoral work at the Free University of West Berlin, the Sorbonne and Oxford University. A specialist in art song literature, Dr. Barr has contributed a number of articles in this area to the recently-published Grove's Music Encyclopedia. Following an extensive teaching career in public and private schools in Pennsylvania, California and Germany, Dr. Barr taught briefly in the New York State University system prior to assuming his present position in Florida.